THE KIDS' WORLD ALMANAC® OF
TRANSPORTATION

THE KIDS' WORLD ALMANAC® OF
TRANSPORTATION

Rockets, Planes, Trains, Cars, Boats, and Other Ways to Get There

BARBARA STEIN

Illustrated by John Lane

WORLD ALMANAC
AN IMPRINT OF PHAROS BOOKS · A SCRIPPS HOWARD COMPANY
NEW YORK

Cover design by Suzanne Reisel
Cover and inside illustrations by John Lane
Interior design by Bea Jackson

First published in 1991.

LIBRARY OF CONGRESS CATALOGING-IN-PUBLICATION DATA
Stein, Barbara.
The kids' world almanac of transportation : rockets, planes, trains,
cars, boats, and other ways to get there / by Barbara Stein : illustrated
by John Lane.
p.   cm.
Includes bibliographical references.
Summary: Describes the varied forms of transportation used by human
beings throughout the ages to get from one place to another.
ISBN 0-88687-490-4 : $14.95. — ISBN 0-88687-491-2 (pbk.) :
$6.95
1. Transportation—juvenile literature.   [1. Transportation.]
I. Lane, John   ill. II. Title.
TA1149.S74   1990   90-41924
629.04—dc20   CIP
AC

Printed in the United States of America

World Almanac
An Imprint of Pharos Books
A Scripps Howard Company
200 Park Avenue
New York, NY 10166

10 9 8 7 6 5 4 3 2 1

Pharos Books are available at special discounts on bulk purchases
for sales promotions, premiums, fundraising or educational use.
For details, contact the Special Sales Department, Pharos Books,
200 Park Avenue, New York, NY 10166

For Carlye, Nichola and Burt,
with love

CONTENTS

ACKNOWLEDGMENTS

No project of this nature could be completed without help. My thanks to the dozens of associations, libraries, archivists, companies, museums and organizations worldwide who so willingly contributed time and information. My special thanks to the following: All-American Soap Box Derby, Boeing Aerospace, Commercial Jets and Helicopters, David Camp, Buddy Carroll, Circus World Museum, Bob Cornish, Eric Castle, *Cycle World* magazine, David Edwards, Flarecraft Corporation, Ford Motor Company, General Motors, Rich Gleason, Goodyear Tire and Rubber Company, Burt Harden, *Hot Rod* magazine, Chris Kugel, *Live Steam* magazine, *Motor Trend* magazine, NASA, Ed Redmond, *Road and Track* magazine, Joe Rice, Mike Ryan, Eileen Schlesinger, Kevin Spaise, Lt. Jane Stevens, Jack Swift, U.S. Navy, U.S. Coast Guard, U.S. Marines, and David Wiggins.

THE KIDS' WORLD ALMANAC® OF
TRANSPORTATION

INTRODUCTION

Transportation— Then and Now

Prehistoric man traveled only as fast as his feet could carry him. Following paths trampled by wild animals, he wandered the earth searching for food and shelter; what little he owned was carried on his back. Thousands of years passed before he tamed the beasts, transferred his goods to *their* backs, and set out to explore the world.

Today it's hard to imagine a world without rockets, planes, trains, cars, and boats. Every second of every day there are millions of vehicles moving people and products all over the earth. This book is stuffed with wacky facts about nearly every vehicle invented to move people over land and sea and into space. You'll find out which ones came first, which are the fastest, and how people the world over get from here to there. So hop aboard and rocket through the ages.

Great Moments in Transportation History

3500 B.C.	The first wheeled vehicles were built by the Mesopotamians.
2700 B.C.	The first system of roads appeared in China.
2500 B.C.	The first ocean-going ship sailed from Egypt.
170 B.C.	The Romans built the first paved streets.
44 A.D.	The wheelbarrow was invented.
1500	Leonardo da Vinci sketched the first flying machines.
1620	The first submarine appeared.
1769	The first steam-powered automobile was built.
1775	The first steamship was launched.
1783	Man flew in an untethered balloon for the first time.
1804	The first successful steam locomotive was introduced.
1815	Macadam (stone) road paving was developed.
1836	The first electric car was tested.
1839	The first bicycle with pedals appeared.
1863	The first successful subway was built.
1885	The first cars with gasoline engines were built.
1903	The first successful engine-powered flight took place.
1906	The first monorail was built.
1930	The jet engine was patented.
1939	The first single-rotor helicopter flew.
1947	Chuck Yeager broke the sound barrier.
1952	The first jetliners entered service.
1954	The first atomic-powered submarine was launched.
1957	The first man-made satellite was launched.
1959	The first Hovercraft glided over the water.
1960	The ''bullet train'' was introduced.
1961	The first manned space flight took place.
1969	The first men landed on the moon.
1970	The first jumbo jet flew across the ocean.
1974	The Concorde SST entered service.
1981	The space shuttle *Columbia* became the first reusable spacecraft.
1990	*Columbia* astronauts captured a satellite that had been in space for six years.

UNIQUE WAYS TO GET THERE

Following is a partial list of some of the most unusual vehicles traveling the world today.

VEHICLE	DESCRIPTION	COUNTRY
Camel Wagons	Covered wagon drawn by camels. Hauls people and goods across the desert.	India

Chinese Wheelbarrow	The single wheel on this large vehicle is placed directly below the load to shoulder the weight. One person pushes and a rope-man or donkey pulls.	China

| **Hansom Cabs** | Horse-drawn carriages with folding tops. City transport and tourist attraction. | United States and Europe |
| **Iceboat** | Pleasure sailboat fitted with runners for speeding over ice, frozen seas, rivers, and lakes. | Northern Europe and United States |

Jaunting Cart or Sidecar	Horse-drawn "touring" carriage. Rider seats are on either side and face outward.	Ireland and England
Chinese Junk	Large boat that doubles as a house, farm, or store.	China
Jeepness	Brightly colored jeep that has been converted to transport about 12 people.	Philippines
Maxitaxi	Minivan used for public transportation that plays calypso music full-blast while drivers drop off riders around town.	Trinidad and Tobago
Ox-Drawn Carts	Open or covered cart drawn by oxen to transport people and goods.	Asia

Pedicabs	Modern version of the rickshaw, a three-wheeled cart pedaled by a driver riding the back portion of a bicycle.	Southeast Asia
Peking Carts	Hooded two-wheeled cart pulled by donkeys.	China
Sampan	Small boat fitted with sails and awnings. Used in harbors and on rivers as floating stores.	China, Japan, and Asia

PASSENGER VEHICLE OLYMPICS

Suppose the world's vehicles got together and staged their own Olympics. Which would be first to cross the finish line? Which would bring up the rear? See for yourself.

VEHICLE	SPEED
Space Shuttle	25,000 miles per hour
Jet Fighter	about 2,200 miles per hour
Concorde SST	1,450 miles per hour

Hydroplane (*Spirit of Australia*)	345 miles per hour
High-Speed Train (French TGV)	322 miles per hour

Indy Race Car	faster than 250 miles per hour
Power Boat ("Texan")	229 miles per hour
Graf Zeppelin	80 miles per hour
Hovercraft (SR-N4 Model)	70 miles per hour
Henry Ford's *Model T*	45 miles per hour
Goodyear Blimp	35 miles per hour
Submarine	35 miles per hour
Aircraft Carrier (U.S.S. *Nimitz*)	35 miles per hour
Ocean Liner (*Queen Mary II*)	31 miles per hour
Clipper Ship	25 miles per hour
Early Steam Locomotive	15 miles per hour
Horse and Buggy	11 miles per hour
Intercity Car	10 miles per hour (average)
Stagecoach	8 miles per hour

TRAVELING AMERICA, YESTERDAY AND TODAY

A trip that today takes only a few hours took days and sometimes months in years gone by. Look below to see how times have changed.

DATE/ VEHICLE	FROM	TO	TIME
1880s			
"Pony Express" Horse	Missouri	California	9 days
Stage-coach	New York	California	1–2 months
Clipper ship	New York	San Francisco	3–4 months
1920s			
Car	San Francisco	New York City	3–3½ months
Train	New York City	Los Angeles	5–6 days
Airplane	New York City	San Diego	1–2 days

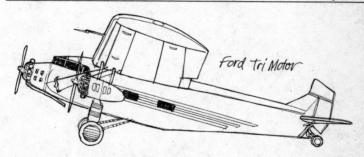

Ford Tri Motor

1990s			
Jetliner	Los Angeles	New York City	4–5 hours
Train	New York City	San Francisco	3–5 days
Car	Los Angeles	New York City	4–5 days
Space shuttle	New York	California	12 minutes

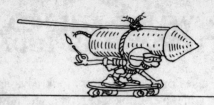

Now read the following chapters to see exactly how we got where we are today and how we'll get where we're going tomorrow. Bon voyage!

CHAPTER 1

Spaceships, Rockets, and Extraterrestrial Vehicles

....

NASA will celebrate its 50th birthday in 2008 and you're invited to the party—in outer space. If all goes as planned, NASA will launch "average citizens" into orbit by the year 2000, and have people living and working in space stations by 2008. Here you'll read about the spaceships that will rocket you to the space stations of the future, and perhaps to colonies to be built on the moon and Mars. You'll find out how astronauts live in weightlessness, all about the space shuttles, far-out facts about rockets, how to become an astronaut, and more.

SPACESHIPS

A Galaxy of Wacky Facts

- *Apollo 8* astronauts used Silly Putty to fasten down their tools in the weightlessness of space. Today, tools are attached with Velcro.
- Famed rocket engineer Wernher von Braun built his first rocket when he was only 12 years old. He strapped a "skyrocket" to his wagon and backed away as the wagon screamed down the street.
- Because the moon's gravity is one-sixth that on Earth, *Apollo* astronauts found it easier and faster to hop than to walk.
- Because there is no up or down in space (due to weightlessness), astronauts can sleep standing up or even upside-down.
- The skull-shaped cap worn under a space helmet is called a "Snoopy cap."
- A lunar spacesuit weighs 180 pounds on Earth but only 30 pounds on the moon.
- *Apollo 11* astronauts were accidentally sent to a lunar crater filled with boulders when NASA miscalculated their landing site on the moon. With only 18 seconds of fuel left for landing, Neil Armstrong manned the controls and landed safely near the moon's Sea of Tranquillity.
- If you'd like to fly in outer space and have $1 million in your piggy bank, Society Expeditions wants to hear from you. "Project Space Voyage" is scheduled for lift-off in the mid-1990s. Passengers will join astronauts and orbit the Earth 16 times a day for three days. Don't forget your camera.
- *Voyager 2* carries on its side a gold-plated record of music and words plus 116 photographs of people and scenes from Earth. The music includes two songs by Beethoven, three by Bach, and Chuck Berry singing "Johnny B. Goode." Sounds include two whales singing, people speaking in 60 different languages, the hiss of bus brakes, and a baby's first cries.
- After brushing their teeth, astronauts must either swallow the toothpaste or spit it into a towel to keep it from floating around the cabin.

- The first person to suggest that rockets could lift people into space was Russian schoolteacher Konstantin Tsiolkovsky in the late 1890s.
- Thirty minutes before touchdown back on Earth, astronauts must inflate their "Anti-G" suits to keep from blacking out. This is because blood drains from the head back into the lower body upon leaving the weightlessness of space.

- Unidentified Flying Objects (UFOs) are reported almost every day. Although some turn out to be clouds, weather balloons, or meteors, not all have been explained. As a result, hundreds of scientists worldwide are studying UFOs. What's more, about 5,600 people belong to the Flying Saucer Club of America.
- The orbiter *Enterprise,* built as a test vehicle in 1976, was named in honor of the U.S.S. *Enterprise* of "Star Trek" fame.
- Since there is no wind or water on the moon, Neil Armstrong's footprints will be there for a very long time.
- Twice now astronauts have carried a human skull into space to find out how much radiation seeps into crew members' heads when they're in space.

- In 1994 NASA plans to sell 40 of the giant external fuel tanks jettisoned by the space shuttle. Who will buy them and how will they be used? One company suggested using them as giant telescopes.
- The age old question, "Is there life on Mars?" was finally answered in 1975 when the *Viking* probes landed on the Red Planet. Although soil tests showed signs of living things, there were no Martians.
- The phrase "the rockets' red glare" in "The Star-Spangled Banner" was inspired by the rockets used by the British to attack Fort McHenry during the War of 1812.

Blast-offs: Firsts in Space

1926 The first successful liquid-propellant rocket was launched by Robert H. Goddard, "the father of modern rocketry."

1957 *Sputnik I*, the world's first artificial satellite, was launched by the Soviets.

1959 *Luna 3*, a Russian space probe, sent back the first pictures of the moon's far side.

1961 Cosmonaut Yuri Gagarin became the first man to travel in space, aboard *Vostok I;* Later that year, Alan B. Shepard became the first American to travel in space.

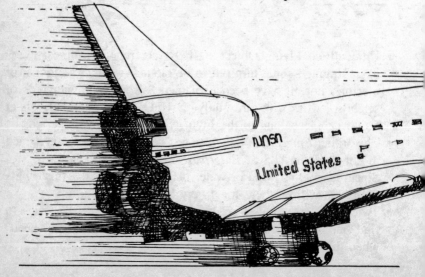

1962 Traveling on the *Friendship 7*, John Glenn became the first American to orbit the Earth. He orbited three times in 4 hours and 55 minutes.

1965 Cosmonaut Aleksei Leonov was first to walk in space. He spent ten minutes outside his spacecraft on a tether; Later that year, Edward H. White became the first American to walk in space. He was attached to an eight-yard long cord and floated for 20 minutes.

1968 *Apollo 7* became the first successful manned launch in Apollo's lunar program; *Apollo 8* orbited the moon ten times carrying three astronauts.

1969 Astronaut Neil Armstrong became the first person to walk on the moon. Stepping out of the lunar module *Eagle,* he put his left foot on the rocky surface. Eighteen minutes later he was joined by Edwin A. Aldrin, Jr. The pair collected rock and soil samples while astronaut Michael Collins piloted the command module *Columbia.*

1975 America's *Apollo 18* and the Soviets' *Soyuz 19* became the first spacecrafts to meet in space. The crews docked 140 miles above the Earth. The U.S. crew included Thomas Stafford, Vance Brand, and Donald Slayton; Soviet cosmonauts included Aleksei Leonov and Valentine Kubason.

1981 The space shuttle *Columbia* became the world's first reusable spacecraft, and orbited the Earth 36 times.

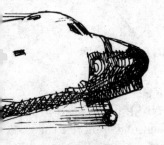

1983 *Challenger*'s first voyage took place on April 4. On June 18 it was launched a second time, carrying the first American woman in space, Sally Ride.

1984 *Challenger* made four historic firsts: It carried the first seven-person crew; demonstrated the first in-space satellite refueling techniques; carried two women for the first time, astronauts Sally Ride and Kathy Sullivan; and Sullivan became the first American woman to walk in space.

1989 On May 4, *Discovery* astronauts launched the unmanned *Magellan* probe on a mission to Venus. It was the first probe to be launched by the shuttle. On August 8, *Columbia* astronauts launched a ten-ton "spy satellite" on a path over the Soviet Union, China and the Middle East. On August 25, after 12 years in space, *Voyager* reached Neptune and sent back live photos to Earth. On December 1, *Solar Max*, a satellite launched in 1980, fell out of orbit and returned to Earth. *Galileo*, a probe headed for Jupiter, was launched. It is expected to reach the planet in 1995 and remain in orbit for two years.

1990 *Columbia* astronauts captured and brought back an 11-ton satellite that had been in space for nearly six years. Their 11-day flight set a record for the space shuttle; *Magellan* reached Venus on August 10 and began orbiting the planet once every three hours. The probe's special radar system photographed the planet's surface and sent images back to Earth. Shuttle astronauts launched the $2 billion Hubble Telescope.

Spaceships of the Future

NATIONAL AEROSPACE PLANE

Imagine flying across country in less than one hour, or to any airport in the world in only three hours. The NASP is expected to fly at more than 12 times the speed of sound and rocket more than 20 miles into the sky to cruise the upper atmosphere. The test plane, called the *X-30*, will make trial flights in the late 1990s. Passengers could be boarded as soon as 2000.

MINI-SHUTTLES

Scientists around the world are designing mini-shuttle orbiters to be launched from the backs of Boeing 747 jetliners. These shuttles are expected to zoom people to the space stations of the future, and to cost less than present-day orbiters.

MAGNETIC PROPULSION SHUTTLE

Michael A. Minovitch, the scientist who created the idea for sending *Mariner 10* and *Voyager 2* into space, has designed a new system for launching spaceships in an electromagnetic tunnel. The 1000-mile tunnel would be dug 46 miles below the Earth's surface. People boarding the space plane would be rocketed through the tunnel, and fly out of a mountaintop and into space within a matter of seconds.

Tomorrow's Spaceports

The National Commission on Space, appointed by President Reagan, hopes to settle colonies of scientists on the moon by 2017, and on Mars by 2027. Here's what they're planning.

SPACE STATION FREEDOM

This $30 billion outpost in space will begin orbiting in late 1999. It will serve as a manned base for scientific experiments and as a spaceport for missions that could take people to Mars. Each of the nine sections, called *modules,* is about the size of a large school bus. It will take 31 flights of the space shuttle to assemble the space station, which is supposed to stay in space for about 30 years.

LUNAR BASE MOON STATION

This station base could be ready as soon as 2000. Its mission is to get things ready for people who will travel to the moon in future years. During test flights, astronauts will experiment with living for long periods in an atmosphere where water and air must be recycled. They'll also roam the moon's surface to make new discoveries, and test the effects of living on the moon's gravity.

MINI–SPACE STATIONS

Some scientists predict that mini–space stations will be used as launch sites for future missions to Mars and other planets. Like *Space Station Freedom,* the stations will stay in orbit, but will be smaller in size and less expensive to build.

Missions and Launches of the Future

NASA is planning more than 100 shuttle missions before 2000. Some missions will last 16 days or longer, so astronauts and scientists have more time to do experiments. One American company has designed an add-on module called a *Spacehab* that will fit behind the crew quarters. This module will provide astronauts with additional work and storage space during long flights.

MISSION TO MARS

The *Mars Observer,* a robot probe, is scheduled for shuttle launch in 1992. The mission's purpose is to map the Red Planet with cameras and then study its surface and gravitational field. A manned mission to Mars is planned for 2020.

MISSION TO PLANET EARTH

A series of unmanned satellites has been planned to help scientists study Earth and to head off possible environmental disasters. One such rocket satellite, *Titan 3,* climbed into space in 1989. Although its payload was secret, experts say its special mission was to guard against nuclear attacks. NASA plans to use *Titan 3*s to launch planetary probes in 1995 and 1996, and to orbit a giant Earth-observing satellite in 1996.

THE PLUTO MISSION

Scheduled for 2015, this mission will be the first to visit the most distant planet in our galaxy, Pluto. Scientists believe the planet is much like Neptune's moon Triton, an icy, rock-filled surface covered by a thin atmosphere.

Five Famous Animalnauts

In the early days of space travel, animals were sent aloft instead of people. The following animals were space pioneers.

Laika, a spacedog, was sent into orbit aboard *Sputnik II* in 1957. He was the first living creature in space. The dog lived inside the pressurized capsule for about a week before its air ran out.

Able and Baker were the first monkeys to survive a launch. They were sent up in a *Jupiter* rocket on May 28, 1959.

Chimpanzees **Ham** and **Enos** were launched on separate flights in 1961. The chimps were trained to pull levers in order to guide their spacecrafts. Enos orbited the Earth twice; Ham's flight lasted only 16½ minutes. Both survived.

How Does the Earth Look from Space?

When asked this question, astronaut William A. Anders replied: "If you can imagine a darkened room with only one clearly visible object, a small blue-green sphere about the size of a Christmas ornament, then you can begin to grasp what the Earth looks like from space."

Far-out Facts

- Astronauts train for spacewalks in a water-filled tank called the "Neutral Buoyancy Simulator." The giant training tank is located at Johnson Space Center in Houston, Texas.
- Many astronauts use motion-sickness medication because the effects of weightlessness make them dizzy.
- Astronauts took a dart game along for recreation during one space flight but couldn't play because the darts floated around in the cabin.
- All together astronauts have spent more than 41,136 hours in space.
- NASA selected a total of 172 astronauts between 1959 and 1987. Today there are 96 men and women in the program.
- *Skylab* astronauts showered in special folding stalls that had a vacuum system to suck out the dirty water. Shuttle astronauts take sponge baths.
- *Pioneer 10,* launched in 1973, is expected to lose contact with the Earth sometime in the 1990s, but will continue gliding through the stars forever.
- Historians believe that rockets were invented by the Chinese in A.D. 1232.
- "Zero-G" or "Zero Gravity" are terms meaning weightlessness. *G* is the force of gravity.
- The most traveled of all space probes are the two *Voyager* probes, which left Earth in 1977. Both have visited Jupiter and Saturn. *Voyager 2* went on to Uranus in 1986, and arrived at Neptune in 1989.
- Eleven women have been in space: U.S. astronauts Sally Ride, Kathryn Sullivan, Rhea Seddon, Shannon Lucid, Anna L. Fisher, Judith A. Resnick, Mary L. Cleave, Bonnie J. Dunbar, Marsha S. Ivins, teachernaut Christa McAuliffe, and Soviet cosmonaut Valentina Tereshkova.
- Twelve Americans have walked on the moon.
- More astronauts have graduated from the U.S. Naval Academy than any other institution—a total of 31.
- John Young has made more space flights than any other astronaut—a total of six.

- *KC-135* is a special NASA airplane that helps astronauts train for weightlessness. During the flights, astronauts can float freely in the cabin for about 30 seconds. It is based at Johnson Space Center in Houston, Texas.
- The *Saturn V* booster rocket is considered the largest and most powerful expendable U.S. launch vehicle ever used for space exploration. Standing 363 feet high, it's longer than a football field and nearly twice the height of the space shuttle (184 feet).
- A spacecraft needs more power to go to the moon than to orbit the Earth. To reach the moon, it speeds about 25,000 miles per hour or about Mach 37. Mach is the speed of sound, about 660 miles per hour.
- If you want to be an astronaut and you're between the ages of 10 and 17, check out the U.S. Space Camp in Huntsville, Alabama. Camp activities include working at Mission Control consoles, operating equipment once used by *Apollo* and *Gemini* astronauts, experiencing weightlessness, and studying astronautics. For more information, write to: Alabama Space and Rocket Center, Huntsville, Alabama, 35806. Phone: 1–800–63SPACE.

What Zero Gravity Does to Your Body

Scientists have been studying the effects of weightlessness on the human body since the first spacecrafts were launched. Here's what they've discovered so far.

1. Body fluids shift from the lower to the upper body and cause a lack of thirst. As a result, astronauts are careful to drink plenty of liquids.
2. Faces grow puffy.
3. Hair sticks straight out and floats around.
4. Beverages taste sweeter.
5. Sniffles and runny noses are a common complaint.
6. Leg muscles tend to grow thinner. Some astronauts call this condition "bird legs."
7. Incredibly, some astronauts grow an inch or more in height.
8. Back on Earth, everything returns to normal.

Outer-Space Experiments for Your Classroom

Would you like to study a lunar rock or grow tomato seeds that have been in outer space? Here are two special NASA programs developed just for kids.

TOMATOES FROM SPACE

In 1990 astronauts retrieved a floating laboratory that had been orbiting Earth for almost six years. One special container was filled with 12.5 million ordinary tomato seeds. What happens to tomato seeds that have been floating in outer space? Will they grow on Earth? How do they compare to seeds that have never been in orbit? You can answer these questions for yourself by asking your teacher to request a special laboratory kit for your classroom. Write to: NASA Seeds Project, Code XEO, NASA Headquarters, Washington, D.C., 20546.

LUNAR ROCKS

What does a lunar rock look like? How is it different from an ordinary rock? If your class would like to study a real lunar rock, ask your teacher to contact the Office of Public Affairs at NASA's

Johnson Space Center in Houston, Texas. The center offers an educational program involving the loan of lunar samples.

The Right Stuff: How to Become an Astronaut

America's pioneering astronauts were jet pilots and engineers. Today, astronauts and mission and payload specialists must have special training in many fields. Here's the training and education you'll need before you apply to NASA.

PILOT-ASTRONAUT

These men and women serve as commanders and pilots (second in command) and fly the spacecraft. Following are the special requirements.

Education College degree in engineering, mathematics, or biological or physical sciences.

Flight Experience One thousand hours of "pilot-in-command" flying time in high-performance jet aircraft.

Physical Requirements *Height:* 5'3" to 6'1". *Vision:* 20/50 or better. *Hearing:* Average or better. *Health:* Excellent.

SCIENTIST-ASTRONAUT

Scientists with training in many fields are chosen to perform experiments during the flights. Although they do not fly the shuttle, they're trained to maneuver the spacecraft in case of emergency. Here's how to qualify.

Education College degree in engineering, biological or physical science, or mathematics, and three years of work experience in the field. Many scientists have advanced degrees from graduate school.

Training Completion of at least 150 hours of special training at the Johnson Space Center in Houston, Texas.

Physical Requirements: *Height:* 5' to 6'3". *Vision:* 20/20 corrected or 20/100 uncorrected. *Hearing:* Average or better. *Health:* Excellent.

Note: Payload specialists are career engineers or scientists selected by their employers or countries to conduct experiments during flights.

The Space Shuttle

If you've ever watched a launch, you know the spacecraft has several different parts. In all, the shuttle has five rocket engines; two solid-fuel boosters mounted on either side, and three liquid-fuel main engines mounted in the rear. The boosters lift the shuttle to an altitude of 28 miles at a speed of 3,095 miles per hour, separate two minutes later, and then return to Earth by parachute. The three main engines provide thrust for six more minutes, and then are shut down. Right now NASA's fleet includes four shuttles: *Columbia,* the oldest and most traveled; *Discovery; Atlantis;* and *Endeavor,* built to replace the *Challenger* and scheduled for lift-off in 1992.

Which is Bigger: The Space Shuttle or Russia's Buran?

Did you know that Russia's space shuttle looks a lot like NASA's orbiter? It's called *Buran,* which means "snowstorm" in Russian. Both of the spaceships are long and sleek with swept-back delta (triangular-shaped) wings and vertical tails. Here's how they compare.

SPACECRAFT	LENGTH	WINGSPAN	DIAMETER
Shuttle	122.2 ft.	78.6 ft.	17 ft.
Buran	119 ft.	79.2 ft.	19 ft.

Shuttle Trivia

- At lift-off the shuttle uses 16,800 gallons of liquid oxygen and about 45,000 gallons of liquid hydrogen each minute.
- The spacecraft can fly from coast to coast in 12 minutes, and from America to Europe in just 20 minutes.
- Since the shuttle does not have its own rocket-powered engines, it's transported back to the launch site by a Boeing 747 Superjet, which carries it piggy-back style.
- The solid rocket boosters, which return to Earth by parachute, land in the Atlantic Ocean and are towed back to the launch center by ships.
- If astronauts have to "ditch" the spacecraft while gliding it to a landing on Earth, they can escape by hooking onto and sliding down a 10½-foot-long "telescoping pole." Once they're away from the shuttle, they can simply parachute to safety.
- The orbiter's wheels are lowered just 14 seconds (about 90 feet high) before touchdown on the runway.
- The giant external tank, which feeds the main engines, is taller than a 15-story building (154 feet high), as wide as a grain silo (27.5 feet wide), and weighs more than 1½ million pounds at lift-off. The tank is released approximately 8½ minutes after launch and then breaks up while re-entering the Earth's atmosphere. The pieces land in the ocean about 58 minutes later.
- The solid rocket boosters provide nearly six million pounds of thrust during the first two minutes of flight.
- Once ignited, the rocket boosters cannot be shut down until all the propellant has burned.

3...2...1 Blast-off: A Typical Countdown and Launch

Six seconds before lift-off: The shuttle's three main engines are started.

Three seconds before lift-off: The shuttle clears the launch tower.

One-third second before lift-off: Solid rocket boosters are fired.

Two minutes after launch: Rocket boosters burn out when the orbiter reaches an altitude of 28 miles and then separate, falling back to Earth and landing in the Atlantic Ocean.

Six and one-half minutes after launch: The shuttle dives from an altitude of 80 miles to about 72 miles to separate the external tank. Crew members feel about three Gs of acceleration.

Eight and one-half minutes after launch: The main engines are shut down, the external tank separates, and then breaks up while returning to Earth.

Ten minutes after launch: The *OMS* (Orbital Maneuvering System) engines burn for about two minutes. These small engines push the shuttle into a two-point path or elliptical orbit around the Earth.

Forty-five minutes after launch: The *OMS* engines fire again and the shuttle is placed into a circular orbit about 200 miles above the Earth.

SOURCE: NASA.

The Crew Module: A Flying House

The crew module, where astronauts live and work, looks like a tall and skinny three-story house. Here's what's inside.

FLIGHT DECK

The top story is where the pilot and commander fly the spacecraft. It looks a lot like the cockpit of a Boeing 747. In all there are 2,020 separate displays, controls, and switches. There are also six windshields, two overhead viewing windows, and two rear-viewing payload bay windows. The pilot's seat is on the right; the commander sits on the left.

MID-DECK

This compartment is the crew's living quarters. It houses the toilet, sleeping stations, kitchen galley, and storage lockers. Astronauts enter the deck through a small circular hatch. Although there's a ladder leading to the flight deck above, hardly anyone uses it; instead, people float up and down through the hatch. A second hatch, called the *airlock hatch,* leads to the cargo area and outside into space. It's in this area that astronauts put on their spacesuits while getting ready for spacewalks.

LOWER DECK

Also called the *payload bay,* this compartment is large enough to hold a school bus, and cargo weighing up to 65,000 pounds. It's here that satellites and laboratories are carried to and from space. It also serves as a work station for scientists. Astronauts lift the cargo in and out of the bay or in and out of space with a 50-foot-long remote manipulator system arm (RMS). The area is reached through removable floor panels.

Space Talk

When astronauts and Mission Control talk to each other they use so many strange words and phrases it's hard to understand what they mean. Here's your own personal guide to understanding this special language.

Abort Stop the launch or mission.
Airlock Small chamber between the flight deck and mid-deck of the orbiter which can be depressurized. Used by crew members while entering or leaving the cabin.

Barbecue Mode Refers to the slow, rolling motion of the spacecraft, which keeps the shuttle from getting too much of the sun's heat on one side.

Cabin Module The crew's living and working quarters aboard the shuttle.

Command Module Shuttle compartment where the crew sits during lift-off and landing.

EMU Extravehicle Mobility Unit, or the spacesuit worn by astronauts during spacewalks and other out-of-shuttle journeys. EMU gear also includes the MMU (see below).

ET External tank that holds the liquid oxygen and hydrogen pumped into the shuttle's main engines. ETs are about 15 stories high (154 feet) and store more than 1½ million pounds of liquid propellant.

EVA ExtraVehicular Activity. Common term for spacewalks and other journeys outside the spacecraft.

G-Force Unit measuring the Earth's gravity at sea level. One G is the force of the Earth's gravity; two Gs are twice that force, and so on.

IVA IntraVehicular Activity. Activities performed inside the spacecraft.

Joystick Control used by crew members to move the orbiter.

Lift-off When the shuttle rockets off the launch pad.

Mains Short for "main engines."

Microgravity Another term for zero gravity or weightlessness.

Mission Control The facilities at Johnson Space Center in Houston where shuttle operations are monitored throughout the flight.

MMU Manned Maneuvering Unit, or the backpack gear that allows astronauts to control their movements while outside the shuttle. The unit is fueled by nitrogen propellant.

NASA National Aeronautics and Space Administration, the agency responsible for America's space program. NASA was established in 1958.

Orbiter The main section of the space shuttle where the cargo and crew are housed.

Pilot Second in command during the flight.

Re-entry When the spacecraft returns to the Earth's atmosphere.

Roger Message received.

Suit Up Put on your spacesuit.
Trajectory The flight path of the spacecraft.
Velocity Another word for speed.
Zero-Gravity Another term for weightlessness.

Suiting Up for Space: Astronaut Clothing

Except for underwear, NASA issues special astronaut clothing before each flight. Of course, since room aboard the shuttle is limited, crew members pack very few items. As a result, socks and shirts are changed only once every three days and trousers are worn for a week. Crew members also receive one jacket and one pair of coveralls. And there's no room for a washing machine.

Flight Coveralls are worn inside the spacecraft, usually by pilots and commanders while flying the shuttle. The coveralls are made of soft navy-blue cotton and are fitted with several pockets. The pockets can be closed with Velcro so nothing escapes during weightlessness.

The spacesuit is worn during the launch and for walks outside the spacecraft. Known as the EMU (ExtraVehicular Mobility Unit), it consists of two separate layers of clothing. The first layer looks like long underwear and has plastic water-filled tubing sewn into the fabric. The fabric is a loose weave, which helps the body breathe. The water-filled tubes cool and regulate the body temperature.

The outer layer is made of a special material that protects astronauts against temperature extremes. It has a built-in unit that provides oxygen for breathing.

The helmet is insulated against extreme temperatures, and is equipped with a light visor. It is worn over a skull-shaped cap that's wired with a transmitter and receiver.

A Day in Outer Space

What can you expect when you're launched into space? How do astronauts cope with day-to-day living when anything that's not nailed down simply floats away? Here's how they've solved some of the problems.

BREATHING

Because the air pumped into the cabin module is much like that on Earth, special breathing equipment is unnecessary. Outside the spacecraft, however, astronauts don their spacesuits, which are equipped with oxygen units.

SLEEPING

Since there is no up or down in space, beds are useless. Instead, astronauts slip into *sleeping restraints,* a sort of sleeping bag that can be anchored to the wall of the cabin. The restraints keep them from floating around while they sleep. In addition, some astronauts wear sleep masks to block out the cabin lights—which burn night and day—and earplugs to deaden the noise. Crew members sleep an average of 8 hours during each 24-hour period and are awakened by Mission Control.

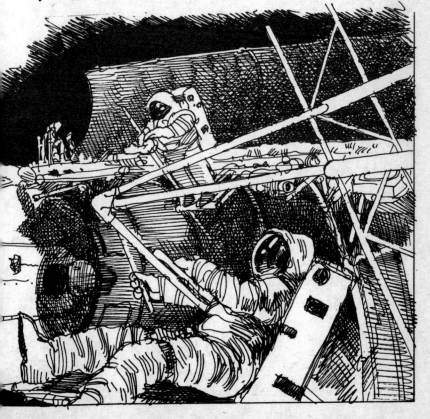

EATING

Since the kitchen galley is too small for a refrigerator or freezer, most foods are prepackaged and precooked. Fresh foods such as fruit and vegetables are consumed in the first few days to keep them from spoiling. Most foods are stored in containers with see-through lids, and marked with colored dots. This is how astronauts know which food is theirs. At mealtime, food is loaded onto aluminum trays and then strapped to the astronaut's knee to keep it in place. Food is speared with knives and forks and eaten normally. After the meal trays are cleaned with "wet wipes," and then stored in closed cabinets. Crew members take in about 2,800 calories a day.

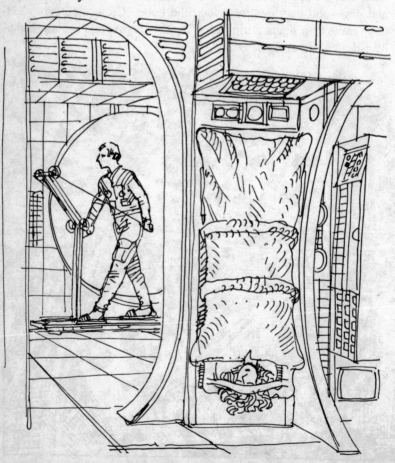

DRINKING
Liquids are sipped through straws to keep the droplets from escaping and floating around.

BATHING
Astronauts are given seven washcloths and three towels for bathing. But since there is no shower or bathtub aboard the shuttle, they take daily sponge baths. *Skylab* crew members, on the other hand, had a special folding shower stall. The stall was equipped with a vacuum system that sucked out the dirty water.

BATHROOM FACILITIES
The shuttle's tiny "bathroom" looks like the toilet on an airplane. But as you can imagine, the biggest problem is simply sitting down and staying on the seat. To solve the problem, astronauts strap on seat belts, push their feet into foot restraints, and grasp the handholds. All waste materials are sucked out with an airstream. During spacewalks, astronauts wear a special device under their spacesuits that collects urine.

EXERCISE
Crew members exercise for 30 minutes every day to keep their muscles strong and toned. But you won't see them doing push-ups or sit-ups. After all, even a baby could do a push-up in weightlessness. Instead, they walk a treadmill device that's anchored to the floor. The device is attached to a special "space belt," a type of shoulder harness that hooks around the waist. Thirty minutes of treadmill walking provides plenty of exercise.

FUN AND GAMES
On long flights astronauts relax by playing games, reading books, and listening to taped music.

DRESSING
Imagine trying to put on your trousers when the pant legs keep floating away. To put on pants astronauts lift both legs at the same time, bring their knees up to their stomachs, hold the trousers away from their bodies, and then quickly push both feet into the pant legs.

Shuttle Firsts

SHUTTLE	LAUNCH DATE	MISSION ACCOMPLISHED
Columbia	4/12/81	First orbital shuttle flight.
Columbia	11/11/82	First commercial satellites launched.
Challenger	4/4/83	First product made in space (microscopic latex spheres).
Challenger	6/18/83	First use of robot arm to retrieve satellite; first American woman in space, Sally Ride.
Challenger	8/30/83	First launch and landing at night; first African American in space, Guion S. Bluford, Jr.
Columbia	11/28/83	First flight of *Spacelab;* first non-American crew member (West German specialist).
Challenger	2/3/84	First "free" spacewalk and use of manned maneuvering unit by Bruce McCandless. First landing at Kennedy Space Center, Florida.
Challenger	4/6/84	First repair of satellite (Solar Maximum) in orbit; altitude record set: 301 miles.
Discovery	8/30/84	First commercial payload specialist, Charles D. Walker; first "frisbee" satellite deployed; first flight of *Discovery*.
Challenger	10/5/84	First seven-person crew; first American woman to walk in space, Kathryn D. Sullivan; first Canadian in space.
Discovery	11/8/84	First retrieval of satellites in orbit.
Discovery	6/17/85	First launch of four satellites; first laser test.
Discovery	8/27/85	First seven-hour spacewalk.
Challenger	10/30/85	First eight-person crew.
Atlantis	11/26/85	First test of building techniques for future space stations; first Mexican in space.
Columbia	1/10/90	First 11-day flight; flight prolonged due to poor weather.

Discovery   4/26/90   First placement of Hubble Telescope, largest scientific instrument ever in space; highest altitude record for shuttle: 381 miles.

SOURCE: NASA.

Space Vehicles You Won't Believe

THE LUNAR ROVER

This amazing $60 million "spacecraft on wheels" was driven by *Apollo* astronauts on the moon's surface. Steered by a type of joy stick, it moves forward and backward like a car. Empty, the rover weighs only 462 pounds, but due to the moon's gravity it can carry up to twice its weight—about 1,140 pounds of Earth weight. Fully loaded, the rover can easily haul two astronauts and their life support systems (about 800 pounds total) and 340 pounds of equipment, tools, and lunar samples. Powered by two 36-volt silver-zinc batteries, the craft can operate for 78 hours, and drive as far as 57 miles without changing batteries. During the last *Apollo* mission, *Lunar Rover 3* set a speed record by traveling 11.1 miles per hour.

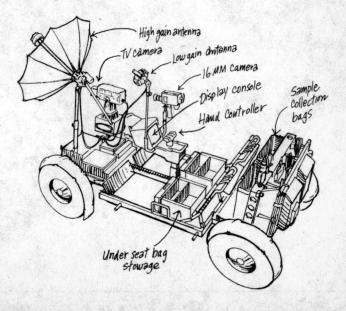

High gain antenna
TV camera
Low gain antenna
16-MM camera
Display console
Hand controller
Sample collection bags
Under seat bag stowage

MANNED MANEUVERING UNIT (MMU)

The MMU looks like a flying chair. It's worn like a backpack over the spacesuit and allows astronauts to jet around outside the shuttle as it orbits. Weighing 255 pounds, it's propelled by nitrogen gas. Astronauts operate the unit with hand controllers built into the armrest. The unit, which can turn in any direction, can operate continuously for 7 hours and 18 minutes.

America's First Super Heroes in Space

The following men were selected in 1959 to become America's first astronauts. Chosen from a field of 500 candidates, each was an experienced fighter pilot with background and training in engineering. And, as NASA required, none were taller than 5', 11". Their pioneering accomplishments are listed below.

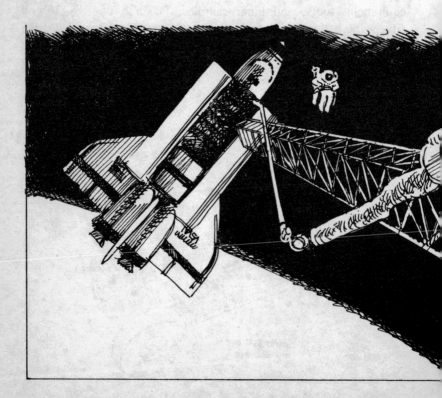

NAME	FIRST FLIGHT	SPACECRAFT	ACCOMPLISHMENT
Alan B. Shepard, Jr.	May 1961	*Freedom 7*	First American in space.
Virgil "Gus" Grissom	July 1961	*Liberty Bell 7*	Second space flight.
John Glenn	February 1962	*Friendship 7*	First American to orbit the Earth.
Scott Carpenter	May 1962	*Aurora 7*	3 Earth revolutions.
Walter Schirra	October 1962	*Sigma 7*	6 Earth revolutions.
L. Gordon Cooper	May 1963	*Faith 7*	22 Earth revolutions.
Donald Slayton	July 1975	*Apollo*	*Apollo-Soyuz* Project.

ROCKETS A TO Z

ATLAS
First flown in 1957, *Atlas* rockets launched the manned *Mercury* flights as well as many satellites and space probes. The rockets stood 82 feet high and developed 430,000 pounds of thrust.

DELTA
These rockets were first launched in 1960. They were successful in lifting payloads weighing up to about 2,500 pounds.

REDSTONE ROCKET
The smallest of America's rocket launchers, the *Redstones* stood 62 feet high and developed 78,000 pounds of thrust. This was the rocket that launched chimpanzees Enos and Ham, and later astronauts Alan Shepard and Virgil Grissom on their famous suborbital (altitude below Earth's orbit) flights during Project *Mercury*.

SATURN
The giants of all American space launchers. *Saturn V* developed a total thrust of about 9 million pounds and stood 10 stories high, 363 feet. *Saturn* rockets sent the *Skylab* crew into orbit and *Apollo* astronauts to the moon.

THOR
Between 1957 and the mid-1960s, *Thor* rockets were used to launch the *Explorer, Pioneer,* and *Discoverer* space probes. They stood 71 feet high and produced about 330,000 pounds of thrust.

TITAN
Titan rockets have lifted probes as well as spacecraft. *Titan 2* lifted the *Gemini* spacecraft while *Titan 3* lifted the *Viking* probes to Mars. In 1990 a *Titan 4* rocket launched the first commercial satellites into space. The rocket stands 160 feet tall and produces 3.5 million pounds of thrust.

V-2 ROCKET

This was the first rocket to travel faster than the speed of sound (about 660 miles per hour at an altitude of 40,000 feet). Developed for the German army by rocket engineer Wernher von Braun, it was first fired in 1942. After World War II, von Braun built rockets for the U.S. Army. The *V-2* is the ancestor of the *Redstone* rocket.

Missions Out of This World

THE HUBBLE SPACE TELESCOPE

Launched by *Discovery* astronauts in 1990, this powerful $2 billion telescope is now 370 miles up into space. Its mission is to orbit the Earth, observe far-off stars, galaxies, and black holes, and watch for changes in our planet for the next 15 years. Ten times more powerful than other telescopes, it can spot the glow of a firefly from 10,000 miles away. The telescope is 43 feet long, 14 feet wide, and weighs more than 22,000 pounds.

SKYLAB

This project put the world's first space station into orbit around the Earth. The first three-man crew orbited for nearly one month, proving that people could live and work in space for long periods of time. The third crew orbited for 84 days, taking thousands of photographs of the Earth and sun. After its third and final mission, the *Skylab* space station remained empty for five years. It broke up while re-entering the Earth's atmosphere in 1979.

APOLLO

In 1961, President Kennedy proposed to Congress that NASA land a man on the moon before the end of the decade. The first manned *Apollo* flight lifted off in 1968, completed ten lunar orbits, and provided America with its first live television broadcast from space. On July 20, 1969, Neil Armstrong became the first man to walk on the moon when the lunar module touched down in the moon's Sea of Tranquility. During the last three *Apollo* flights, astronauts explored the moon's surface with a lunar rover vehicle and brought back to Earth loads of rock samples.

GEMINI

The goal of the *Gemini* Project was to see if two people could live in space for two weeks or longer. The *Gemini* capsule was larger and heavier than *Mercury*'s, and the crew's re-entry module was fitted with two sets of engines. During its ten missions, *Gemini* astronauts made four famous firsts: spacewalks, totaling 12 hours, 12 minutes; docking in space, nine times; manned orbital rendez-vous, ten times; and set a world altitude record. *Gemini*'s success helped NASA put the first man on the moon.

MERCURY

America's first manned space program and the one for which the original seven astronauts were selected in 1959. Project *Mercury* had two goals: (1) to see if people could live and work in space, and (2) to develop space technology for future manned flights. The first *Mercury* mission launched Alan B. Shepard, Jr., into subor-bital flight in 1961, making him the first American in space. The final *Mercury* flight was piloted by L. Gordon Cooper in 1963. After orbiting the Earth 22 times in just 34½ hours, Gordon proved that people could survive in space for at least one day.

Unmanned Missions to the Planets

GALILEO

Galileo, named after the seventeenth-century discoverer of Jupiter's moon, was launched by the space shuttle *Atlantis* in October 1989. The spacecraft is expected to reach Jupiter in 1995, and to orbit the planet for two years. A robot is scheduled to separate from the spacecraft and parachute through the planet's atmosphere. By studying Jupiter, scientists hope to learn more about the birth of the solar system.

MAGELLAN

Magellan was launched on a mission to Venus by *Atlantis* astro-nauts in August 1989. Equipped with sophisticated radar, it mapped the cloudy planet and revealed never-before-seen details of its surface. Because Venus makes only one revolution for every 243 Earth days, the probe took nearly eight months to map the planet.

VOYAGER

Voyager 1 passed Jupiter in 1979 and Saturn in 1980 and made discoveries about both planets and their moons.

Voyager 2 passed Jupiter in 1979, Saturn in 1981, and Uranus in 1988, sending back thousands of photos. In 1989, it passed closest to Neptune—about 3,000 miles above the planet—before heading for its largest moon, Triton. *Voyager 2* gave the world never-before-seen information. Scientists discovered that the Blue Planet has five rings and three moons. Today the spacecraft is headed out of the solar system. Its electrical power is expected to wink out in 2015.

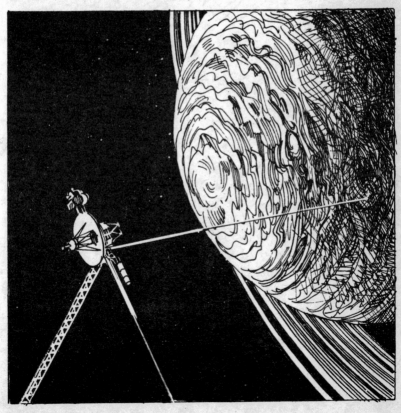

VIKING

Viking I and *Viking II* landed on Mars in 1976, sending back photos and scientific data about the Red Planet.

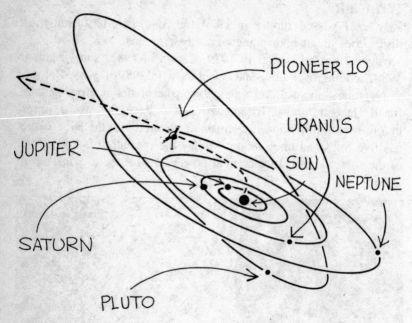

PIONEER

Pioneer 10 explored Jupiter in 1973, and in 1983 it became the first spacecraft to escape the solar system.

Pioneer-Saturn flew past Jupiter in 1974, and passed Saturn in 1979, sending back photos and information about both planets.

In 1978, *Pioneer Venus 1* began orbiting Venus, and *Pioneer Venus 2* entered Venus's atmosphere to measure its density.

MARINER

Mariner 4 photographed Mars in 1965, and measured conditions in space.

Mariner 9 orbited Mars and sent back photos in 1971.

In 1973, *Mariner 10* was the first probe to fly past two planets, Venus and Mercury.

Five Spaceports You Can Visit

If you've wondered what goes on inside America's space centers, wonder no more. The following spaceports offer special tours, exciting exhibits, and more for kids and parents.

AMES RESEARCH CENTER

Moffet Field, California The scientists working in this center are studying the possibility of life on other planets and the effects of space travel on humans. This facility serves as Mission Control for the *Galileo* probe.

JOHN F. KENNEDY SPACE CENTER

Cape Canaveral, Florida America's main spaceport, and the primary launch and recovery site for the space shuttle. This facility houses the 52-story high "Vehicle Assembly Building," where the solid rocket boosters and external fuel tanks are attached, a building for servicing and repairing the orbiter, and two launch pads. The huge center is spread over 84,000 acres of ground.

JOHNSON SPACE CENTER

Houston, Texas Mission Control, the people who oversee and monitor the spacecraft from lift-off to landing, is located at this facility. The center also houses the astronaut training program, including flight simulators and neutral buoyancy tanks. It is named in honor of former president Lyndon B. Johnson.

GODDARD SPACE FLIGHT CENTER

Greenbelt, Maryland NASA's scientific satellites (weather, communications, and navigation) are designed, operated, and tracked at this center. Opened in 1959, it is named in honor of rocket pioneer Robert Goddard.

MARSHALL SPACE FLIGHT CENTER

Huntsville, Alabama Scientists working in this facility are developing rocket launchers as well as spacecraft. Marshall scientists developed the *Skylab, Saturn* launch vehicles, and the shuttle's engines. Named after General George C. Marshall, the center was opened in 1960.

CHAPTER 2

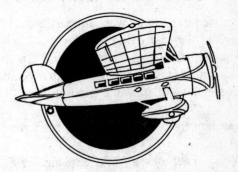

Airplanes and Other Flying Machines

. . . .

People have dreamed of flying for centuries. Ancient legends are filled with myths of winged gods, winged horses, winged men, and even flying carpets. Finally, in the 1500s, Leonardo da Vinci of Italy sketched the first flying machines; his "ornithopoter" had flapping wings. But two hundred years passed before man finally soared with the birds—in a balloon constructed of paper and cloth.

In this chapter you'll read about the hypersonic planes of tomorrow, the biggest, fastest, and most powerful supersonic jets of today, the warbirds of yesterday, and all about the pioneering daredevils who strapped wings to their arms, leaped from buildings and clifftops, and flapped their way into history.

AIRPLANES

A Cockpit of Wacky Facts

- The first "passengers" to fly were animals: a duck, a rooster, and a sheep were in the first flying balloon.
- When the balloon *Globe* was launched in Paris in 1783, it rose into the sky and vanished. When it finally landed in a tiny village, people thought it was a monster and "killed" it with pitchforks.
- In 1990 President Bush banned broccoli from Air Force One, the presidential jet.
- Because birds sometimes fly into airplanes, the Air Force has developed a "chicken gun" to see how the birds affect the plane. This 20-foot-long cannon shoots dead chickens onto the plane's windshield, landing gear, and engines.
- The cockpit of *Voyager,* the first plane to fly around the world without refueling, was so small that only one person could enter at a time. Thus pilots Dick Rutan and Jeana Yeager took turns at the controls.
- During his 1989 flight over the North Pole, Air Force pilot Charles Mack navigated with a homemade sundial.
- The *SR-71 Blackbird,* a spy plane, was originally named the *RS-71.* The name was changed when President Lyndon Johnson accidentally mixed up the letters, calling it the *SR-71.*
- Jet routes are highways in the sky. Odd-numbered routes travel north and south; even-numbered routes travel east and west.
- The Wright brothers (the first to fly an engine-powered plane) owned and operated a bicycle repair shop.
- The OS2U *Kingfisher,* an early carrier-based fighter, could not land on a ship's deck. Equipped with boat-like floats, it landed on the water and was lifted aboard by a crane.
- The Caterpillar Club is a group of people who have survived disaster by parachuting out of airplanes.
- In 1982 a jetliner accidentally became the world's heaviest glider. Ash from an erupting volcano rose 37,000 feet and shut down the jet's engines. Luckily, pilots were able to restart the engines and went on to land safely. None of the 260 passengers were hurt.

• Germany's famed "Red Baron" (Manfred von Richtofen) was so named because his Fokker Triplane was painted bright red. He was shot down in 1918 by a Sopwith Camel piloted by Roy Brown of England.

• Famed World War I flying ace Eddie Rickenbacker began his military career as a general's chauffeur.
• In the 1930s the Royal Typewriter Company advertised its portable typewriters by dropping them to the ground by parachute.
• Douglas "Wrong Way" Corrigan earned his nickname when he landed in Ireland instead of California. He claimed to have read his compass backward, flying across the Atlantic Ocean rather than across the United States.
• Chuck Yeager named the first Bell XS rocket plane *Glamorous Glennis,* after his wife.
• According to some historians, the first people to fly were Chinese criminals who were lifted into the air by kites.
• Because early airliners also carried the mail, some passenger "seats" were actually lumpy sacks of mail.

Firsts in Flight

1782 The first balloon was sent into the air by the Montgolfier brothers of France. It rose 6,000 feet and floated for ten minutes.

1783 The first manned balloon flight was made by J. F. Pilâtre de Rozier of France. He died two years later when one of his balloons exploded. His death marked the first air disaster.

1785 The parachute was invented by Frenchman Jean-Pierre Blanchard.

1793 The first American balloon flight was made over Philadelphia by Jean-Pierre Blanchard, who floated for 45 minutes before landing in New Jersey.

1848 The first steam-powered model plane was flown over the Potomac River by Englishman John Stringfellow. The plane flew 120 feet and crashed in the water.

1852 Frenchman Henri Giffard built and flew the first power-driven balloon, a 145-foot-long dirigible powered by steam. He sped 6.7 mph from Paris, France, to Trappe, France.

1853 Sir George Cayley built the first successful airplane, a glider. Cayley was 80 years old at the time and sent his coachman aloft. The terrified coachman quit his job after the flight.

1891 Otto Lilienthal of Germany was first to pilot a glider successfully. He stood on a cliff and flapped into the wind.

1900 Count Ferdinand von Zeppelin of Germany built the first practical rigid airship, the *Zeppelin*.

1903 Brothers Orville and Wilbur Wright made the first engine-powered heavier-than-air flight in *Flyer,* a biplane. Orville was first to pilot the plane because he won the toss of a coin. He traveled 120 feet in 12 seconds.

1907 The first manned helicopter, *Gyroplane No. 1,* which was tied to the ground, whirled into the air carrying French brothers Louis and Jacques Breguet; the first free flight was made in a twin-rotor model built by Paul Cornu of France.

1910–11 The first commercial airliner, a dirigible, flew between German cities; Glenn Curtiss invented the hydroplane, a flying boat.

1913–14 Russian inventor Igor Sikorsky built and flew the first four-engine plane, *The Grand*; America's first scheduled airliner, a Benoist flying boat, flew between St. Petersburg, Florida, and Tampa, Florida. The airliner lasted only a few months.

1923–30 Spaniard Juan de la Cierva made the world's first successful autogyro flight in *Cierva C-6,* which looked like an airplane with helicopter rotors; Englishman Sir Frank Whittie invented the jet-propelled engine.

1939–40 The Heinkel Company of Germany built the first jet-propelled airplane; Russian immigrant Igor Sikorsky built and flew the first practical single-rotor helicopter, in Stratford, Connecticut.

1947 Air Force Captain Charles "Chuck" Yeager broke the sound barrier in the Bell XS-1 rocket plane.

1952 The world's first jet passenger service was flown by the De Havilland Comets, in England.

1962–67 Air Force Major Robert White made the first airplane flight into space in the X-15 rocket, flying more than 50 miles above the earth; the X-15A rocketed 4,520 mph (Mach 6.72) and set a record as the world's fastest fixed-wing aircraft.

1970 The first jumbo jet, the Boeing 747, entered service in America.

1976 The Concorde SST, developed in France and England, began international passenger service between Europe and the United States.

1989 The Air Force introduced the B-2 *Stealth* Bomber, a $500 million single-seater warplane and claimed it could not be detected by radar; the A320 "fly-by-wire" jetliner, which automatically detects and corrects problems in flight, was introduced in Europe.

1990 The MD-11, a wide-body jetliner, was test-flown. It was the first three-engine jet introduced in 20 years.

Superjets of Tomorrow

If you like speed, you'll love the new superjets. Aircraft engineers are designing jets that will fly faster, carry heavier loads, and make less noise than modern-day planes. Here are some of the designs now on the drawing boards.

HYPERSONIC FLYER

Imagine hurling through the air at eight times the speed of sound at altitudes up to 25 miles above the Earth. Hypersonic jets will be powered by rocket engines for reaching speeds up to Mach 8 (eight times the speed of sound), and then switch to "scramjets" to zoom even faster. Scientists believe passengers will feel like they're being launched into orbit. Watch for it in 2000.

ELECTRIC COMMUTER JET

Batman would love this flying machine. Shaped like a flying saucer, it will be powered by electricity, glide through the air without making a sound, and take off and land like a helicopter.

ADVANCED SUPERSONIC TRANSPORT

The new SSTs will fly at twice or three times the speed of sound

and carry twice the number of people as the Concorde, about 200 passengers. One model has been designed with a "swing wing," a wing that can change position during flight. Plan on boarding this superjet in the near future.

THE ELECTRIC FLIVVER
If you like flying cars, you'll love the *Flivver*. This autogyro has helicopter-like rotors that whirl around the car's body; the craft takes off and lands like a chopper. On the ground the vehicle will be powered by an electric motor and drive like any other car. The rotors are removable.

THE BOEING 777
This wide-body twin-jet airliner will seat 375 passengers. Watch for it in 1995.

THE X-29
Aircraft designers have been experimenting with different wing designs for decades. Swept back "delta wings" and "swing wings" have proved to reduce drag. But the wings on the *X-29* military fighter will be slanted forward. The plane is scheduled to debut before 2000.

Fast, Faster, Fastest

Following are some of the world's fastest aircraft.

ROCKET-ENGINE
The *X-15A-2*, which rocketed to nearly Mach 7 (4,520 miles per hour) in 1967. It was piloted by Air Force Major William J. Knight.

SPY PLANE
The *SR-71 Blackbird*, with a top speed faster than Mach 3, and a cruising altitude above 19 miles. First built in 1966, it was grounded in 1990 and is now on display at the Smithsonian Institution in Washington, D.C.

U.S. BOMBER
The *FB-11A*, with a top speed of Mach 2.5.

AIRLINER
The Concorde, with a cruising speed of Mach 2.2 (1,450 miles per hour). In 1983, the Concorde whizzed passengers from New York to London, England, in less than three hours. The plane carries 110 passengers.

BIPLANE
The Italian *Fiat C.R. 42B*, which sped 323 miles per hour in 1941.

Plane Trivia

- The world language of pilots is English. This means that *all* pilots and air traffic controllers must speak English, even if they don't work in English-speaking countries.
- It takes about 45 gallons of paint to put the average airline color scheme on a Boeing 737.
- The first official U.S. public airplane flight was made in July 1908 by Glenn Curtiss in his plane the *June Bug*.
- Airline pilots flying across the country may be directed by as many as 30 different air traffic controllers.

AIRPLANES AND OTHER FLYING MACHINES

- The Boeing 747-300 jumbo jet can carry up to 500 passengers.
- The world's longest runway, 19 miles, is Rogers Dry Lake at Edwards Air Force Base, California. The main strip is 7 miles long and an emergency strip extends another 12 miles.
- The Concorde's pointed nose can be swung up or down. Pilots shift the nose down to have a better view of the runway and a clearer view during takeoffs and landings. During supersonic flights, they swing the nose upward to reduce drag.
- The term *Mach* refers to the speed of sound. At altitudes of 35,000 feet, sound travels 660 miles per hour; at sea level, it travels 740 miles per hour.
- The first airmail service was flown by U.S. Army pilots in 1918.
- The world's busiest airport is Chicago's O'Hare International, where planes take off or land about every 39 seconds around the clock.
- In 1925 Henry Ford manufactured a three-engine plane called the Ford Trimotor. Although it was a popular airliner, the plane was so noisy that passengers stuffed cotton balls in their ears.
- The shortest scheduled airline flight is made three times daily by a Boeing 727, between San Francisco and Oakland, California, a distance of 12 miles.
- If you want a smooth ride on a passenger jet, sit on or just forward of the wing. For the bumpiest ride, sit in the tail section.
- *Big Texas*, considered the world's largest hangar, is located at Kelly Air Force Base in Texas. Each door is as tall as a five-story building (60 feet high), and measures 250 feet wide.
- The Boeing 747 Manufacturing Plant in Everett, Washington, covers 47 acres of ground and is considered the largest building in America.
- *Enola Gay* was the famous American warplane that dropped the atom bomb on Hiroshima, Japan, during World War II.
- "Floatplanes," "flying boats," and "amphibians" are types of seaplanes that can take off and land on water.
- The Blue Angels, the Navy's demonstration flying team, perform in the *F/A-18 Hornet*. The Air Force's Thunderbirds perform in the *F-16 Fighting Falcon*.
- The first woman to break the sound barrier was Jacqueline Cochran, in an *F-86 Sabre,* in 1953.

- Boeing is the world's largest producer of commercial jetliners.
- The four forces that control flight are gravity, lift, drag, and thrust.

Amazing Kid Pilot

Tony Aliegena, a sixth grader from California, has set several world records. Here are some of his accomplishments.

Age 4   Tony began learning to fly.

Age 9   In March 1988 he flew alone for the first time and became the world's youngest person to solo.

Age 9   In April 1988, he flew across the United States, breaking a world record set by ten-year-old Eric Fiederer.

Age 11   In 1989 Tony amazed the world by flying 19,000 miles to the Soviet Union and around the world in a single-engine *Cessna 210 Turboprop*. Tony was accompanied by his ten-year-old Soviet pen pal, Roman Tcheremnykh, his parents, and an observer from the National Aeronautic Association.

The President's Flying Palaces

Air Force One, the president's jet, is a specially built Boeing 747. And there are two of them. Costing $650 million to develop, they

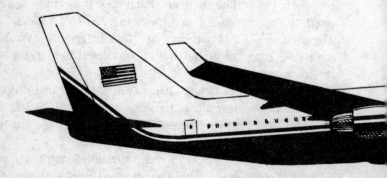

are the most expensive transport planes ever built. Each is crewed by 23 people (pilots, navigators, stewards), carries up to 70 passengers, and is equipped with the fanciest radar and anti-missile devices available. Delivered in 1990, these "flying palaces" have features not found in most houses. Here's what's inside:

6 bathrooms	85 telephones
1 fireproof safe	4 computers
1 pressroom with TV monitors	One 6-channel stereo system
2 copying machines	2 conference rooms
Several crew bunks and sleeper chairs	2 refrigerator-freezers, which can pack enough food to feed crew
2 kitchen galleys	and passengers for a week.

The special presidential suite, located up front, has twin beds, a shower-tub combination with electric window curtains, and medical hookups built into the ceiling in case the president falls ill.

Super Choppers, a small fleet of *Sikorsky VH-60* helicopters, are ready whenever the president needs them. The choppers are used for short hops between cities and around town, for trips to and from the airport, as transport to and from aircraft carriers, and for observing natural disasters.

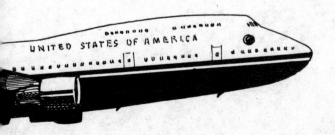

Ghosts of the Sky

THE GHOST BLIMP

The two-man crew of *America,* a Navy blimp, suddenly disappeared while performing routine antisubmarine patrols over the Pacific Ocean in the 1950s. The pilots radioed that they had spotted an oil slick and were going down to investigate. That was the last anyone heard from them. Later that day the blimp drifted inland toward San Francisco, California, and finally landed. But when rescuers stepped inside, the crew had vanished. To this day no one knows what happened.

THE AMELIA EARHART MYSTERY

In 1937 famed aviator Amelia Earhart and navigator Fred Noonan set out to fly around the world. Everything went well until the last leg of the trip, when the plane suddenly disappeared from the sky. The last radio transmission put the aircraft about 1,800 miles southwest of Hawaii. Since that time hundreds of people have searched for the wreckage and tried to figure out what went wrong. Some people believe that Earhart was a spy and disappeared on purpose. Others say she landed safely on a far-off island and became a princess. Most people believe her plane crashed and now rests on the bottom of the ocean.

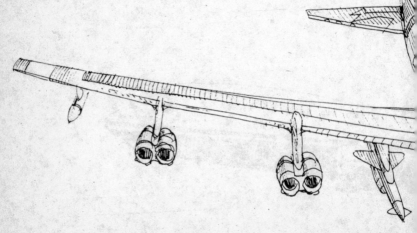

THE GHOST SQUADRON

Don't be alarmed if you see a pack of World War II fighters flying over your house. It's the Confederate Air Force, a group of World War II pilots whose "ghost squadron" includes more than 100 historic warplanes. Their fleet includes the *P-51 Mustang* (fighter), the *Avenger* (torpedo bomber), and the awesome *B-17 Flying Fortress*. Based in Texas, the squadron performs in air shows nationwide.

Aircraft Bests

MOST POWERFUL U.S. TRANSPORT

The *C-5 Galaxy*, which hauls rocket parts for NASA. With its giant flip-up nose, the plane can load and fly with more than 400 tons of cargo, or about 16 trucks, 3 battle tanks, and 5 attack helicopters.

HEAVIEST BOMBER

The Boeing *B-52H Stratofortress*, which can haul 244 tons of cargo, a weight equal to 40 large elephants. This eight-jet bomber carries 12 attack missiles or 24 750-pound bombs under its wings. Its belly can hold 84 500-pound bombs and 8 extra missiles.

LARGEST AIRLINER

The Boeing 747 Jumbo Jet, which can carry up to 500 passengers at a maximum speed of 620 miles per hour. The wing area is larger than a basketball court (5,500 square feet) and the tail height is as high as a six-story building.

LARGEST WINGSPAN

The *Spruce Goose,* with a wingspan longer than a football field, 320 feet. Designed and built by millionaire Howard Hughes in the 1940s, the plane has eight propellers and tips the scales at 213 tons. Hughes flew the plane only once. On November 2, 1947, he lifted it 70 feet off the ground and cruised a total distance of 1 mile. It's now a walk-through museum in Long Beach, California.

HIGHEST FLIER

A Russian *MIG-25*, which set a world altitude record by soaring more than 23 miles into the air, in 1977.

SMALLEST AIRPLANE

Birdman TL-1, a monoplane weighing only 100 pounds. It was first flown in Florida in 1975.

MOST POWERFUL PISTON-ENGINE PLANE

The *B-36 Superbomber,* built in 1950. This bomber could carry a load of bombs weighing 10,000 pounds for distances up to 10,000 miles without refueling.

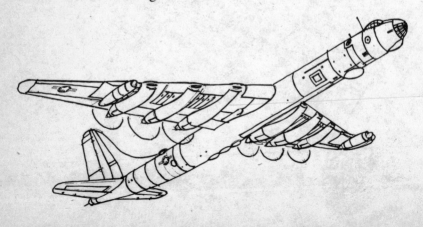

Flying Flops

Inventors have created all sorts of funny contraptions so people could fly. Here are three of the silliest flying machines ever invented.

THE GOODYEAR INFLATOPLANE

If you can blow up a rubber raft, why not an airplane? The *Inflatoplane* was supposed to be carried in a soldier's overnight bag or dropped to pilots who had parachuted to the ground. The idea was simply to blow up the plane, hop into the open cockpit, and fly away. Although the plane could reach speeds up to 55 miles per hour, the idea never caught on.

THE FLYING FLAPJACK

This round stubby-winged plane looked like a pancake fitted with propellers. Built in the 1940s, it was designed to serve the Navy as a carrier-based attack plane. The *Flapjack* could hover like a helicopter and fly in a straight line at speeds faster than 500 miles per hour. It never caught on.

THE WATERMAN ARROWBILE

Take a small car, slap a propeller on the back, add a pair of wings, and you have the *Waterman Arrowbile*. The craft was designed for vacationing families. Pilot-drivers could drive it to the airport, take off from the runway, fly to the next city, and then sight-see along the road or in town. The tail and wings could be removed for road use. A good idea that never caught on.

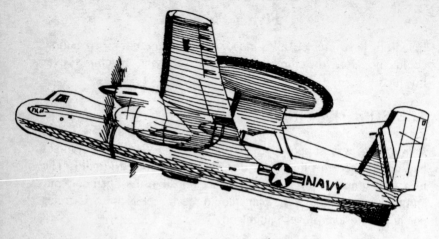

Awesome Airplanes

E-2 HAWKEYE and AWACS

Few military planes take a back seat to the *Hawkeye*, the Navy's early warning aircraft, or the Air Force's *AWACS* (Airborne Warning and Control System) plane. These planes are equipped with giant 24-feet-in-diameter disc-shaped radar platforms that ride piggyback atop the planes. Armed with thousands of pounds of electronic equipment, they can automatically track more than 600 targets, control about 40 airplanes, and jam enemy radar all at the same time. Both planes can stay airborne for more than nine hours without refueling.

LEAR JET

The Cadillac of private jets, the plush *Lear* has all the comforts of home and then some. This jet has set dozens of performance records over the years.

In 1976, a world speed record was set by *Lear* by flying around the world in just 48 hours and 48 minutes, at an average speed of 440.23 miles per hour.

In 1979, a *Lear* jet flown by astronaut Neil Armstrong set four world speed records for aircraft of its class: two for altitude, one for sustained flight at 51,000 feet, and one for high-altitude climbs.

GOSSAMER CONDOR

Designed in 1977 by Drs. Paul MacCready and Peter Lissaman of California, the *Gossamer Condor* was the world's first successful man-powered airplane. Built of thin aluminum tubing covered with plastic, it has a wingspan of 96 feet. During its first record-breaking flight, Bryan Allen, a bicycling champ, pedaled the plane 1.15 miles in 7 minutes 27.5 seconds, at speeds up to 10 miles per hour. The plane now hangs in the National Air and Space Museum in Washington, D.C.

STEARMAN KAYDET

Nicknamed "Old Smokey," this colorful biplane stars in many national air shows. With its red-and-white checkered nose and tail, it is easy to spot. Stunt fliers often ride or walk the wings while pilots perform loops, stall turns, and fly upside-down over the runway at speeds up to 100 miles per hour. It was designed by Lloyd Stearman in the late 1920s.

Famous Firsts

FIRST MAN-POWERED INTERNATIONAL FLIGHT

Pedaling the *Gossamer Albatross*, pilot Bryan Allen crossed the English Channel (22 miles) at speeds up to 15 miles per hour and altitudes ranging from 6 inches to 25 feet above the water. Flight time: 2½ hours.

LONGEST MAN-POWERED FLIGHT

Glenn Tremmi of Connecticut flew 37 miles in the *Michelob Light Eagle* over Edwards Air Force Base, California, in 1987. Flight time: 2 hours, 13 minutes.

FIRST INTERNATIONAL SOLAR-POWERED FLIGHT

Dr. Paul MacCready's 210-pound *Solar Challenger,* piloted by Steve Ptacek across the English Channel, from Paris to Kent, England, in 1981. Flight time: 5 hours, 23 minutes.

FIRST NONSTOP TRANSPACIFIC FLIGHT

Majors Clyde Pangborn and Hugh Herndon in *Miss Veedol,* in 1931, from Japan to Washington. Flight time: 41 hours, 13 minutes.

FIRST SOLO OVER THE POLE

Charles F. Blair, over the North Pole, from Norway to Fairbanks, Alaska, in 1951. Flight time: 10 hours, 29 minutes.

EARLIEST POLAR FLIGHT

Admiral Richard E. Byrd and Floyd Bennett, in a Fokker *Trimotor,* from Kingsbay, Spitsbergen, over the North Pole and back, in 1926. Flight time: 15½ hours.

Pilot Talk

Ailerons Wing flaps that help the aircraft turn.

ATA Actual time of arrival, figured during the flight as the aircraft passes each checkpoint.

ATC Air Traffic Controller, person who oversees flight of the aircraft from the ground.

Altimeter Instrument that measures height above the ground.

Automatic Pilot Instrument that flies the aircraft automatically.

Clearance Delivery Frequency Radio frequency used by pilots to check altitudes and jet routes.

Cleared OK, for landing or takeoff.

Cleared as Filed Pilot's flight plan has been accepted as is.

ETA Estimated time of arrival, figured by pilots before takeoff.

Flight Level Shorthand for *altitude*. A pilot flying at 31,000 feet would report his altitude as "flight level 310."

Flight Recorder Also known as the "black box." Details of each flight are recorded by this device and replayed after crashes.

Hand-off The act of transferring pilots from air controller to air controller during flights.

Hold Short Stop at a certain place, such as just before entering or crossing a runway.

Payload Total load carried, including passengers and cargo.

Position and Hold Roll onto the runway, but do not take off.

SARAH Search and rescue and homing. This is the radio transmitter on a pilot's life jacket.

Three-Point Landing Normal landing position where all three wheels touch down at the same time.

Taxi Proceed slowly.

Vector Heading. Usually spoken as question when pilot asks for headings to a specific location, such as "Vector to New York?"

Victor Airways Altitudes of less than 18,000 feet.

Pilot Codes

To make sure there are no mix-ups over the air waves, pilots substitute words for each letter of the alphabet. An aircraft whose call letters are ATD, for example, would be reported as "Alpha Tango Delta."

A	Alpha	J	Juliette	R	Romeo
B	Bravo	K	Kilo	S	Sierra
C	Charlie	L	Llama	T	Tango
D	Delta	M	Mike	U	Uniform
E	Echo	N	November	V	Victor
F	Foxtrot	O	Oscar	W	Whiskey
G	Golf	P	Pappa	X	X-ray
H	Hotel	Q	Quebec	Y	Yankee
I	India		(*K-beck*)	Z	Zulu

COMPASS CODES

Pilots substitute numbers for words when giving or receiving directions. A plane turning north, for example, would be turning "360."

360 means *north*   270 means *west*
180 means *south*   090 means *east*

Record-Breaking Flights

Thousands of aviation records have been set over the years. The following is a partial list of some of the most famous pilots and their aircraft to ever fly around the world, across the oceans, and from coast to coast across the U.S. Record-breaking times are sometimes reported in days and sometimes in hours to make the record more newsworthy, or seem faster.

Around the World

FIRST NONSTOP WITHOUT REFUELING
Voyager, a lightweight plane built and piloted by Jeana Yeager and Dick Rutan in 1986. *Voyager* weighed only 8,934 pounds, carried 1,240 gallons of fuel, and averaged 115.6 miles per hour. Flight time: 216 hours, 3 minutes, 44 seconds.

FASTEST NONSTOP
Three U.S. Air Force *B-52s,* averaging 525 miles per hour, in 1957. Flight time, with four mid-air refuelings: 45 hours, 19 minutes.

FIRST WOMAN
Geraldine Mock in *Spirit of Columbus,* in 1984. Flight time: 29 days, 11 hours.

FIRST NONSTOP
Lucky Lady II, a Boeing *B-50 Superfortress,* flown by Air Force Captain James Gallager and a crew of 13 men, in 1949. Flight time, with four mid-air refuelings: 3 days, 22 hours, 1 minute.

FIRST SOLO

Wiley Post in *Winnie May,* a Lockheed *Vega,* in 1933. Flight time, in ten hops: 7 days, 18 hours, 40 minutes.

EARLIEST

The *Chicago* and the *New Orleans,* two Army biplanes, in 1924. Flight time, with 52 stops: nearly six months. Actual flying time: 363 hours, 7 minutes.

Across the Atlantic

FASTEST

The *SR-71 Blackbird,* flown by Majors James Sullivan and Noel Widdifield, in 1974. Flight time: 1 hour, 54 minutes, 56 seconds. Average speed: faster than 1,806 miles per hour.

FASTEST SOLO CROSSING
Captain John J. A. Smith in a Rockwell 685, in 1978. Flight time: 8 hours, 47 minutes.

FIRST NONSTOP JET CROSSING
Air Force Colonel David Schilling, from England to Maine, in 1950. Flight time: about 10 hours.

FIRST NONSTOP SOLO
Charles Lindbergh in *The Spirit of St. Louis,* a monoplane, from New York to Paris, in 1927. Flight time: 33½ hours.

FIRST WOMAN SOLO
Amelia Earhart in a Lockheed *Vega,* from Newfoundland to Ireland, in 1932. Flight time: 15 hours, 18 minutes.

EARLIEST CROSSING
Lieutenant Commander Albert Read and his crew, from New York to England, in a Curtiss *Flying Boat,* in 1919. Flight time: 58 hours, 58 minutes.

EARLIEST NONSTOP
British Captain John Alcock and Lieutenant Arthur Brown in a *Vicker's Vimy,* from Newfoundland to Ireland, in 1919. Flight time: 15 hours, 57 minutes.

Across the United States

FASTEST JET
The *SR-71 Blackbird,* which on its final flight in 1990 crossed the United States in just 68 minutes, 17 seconds, shattering the old record by 2½ hours. Average speed: 2,112.53 miles per hour.

FASTEST BOMBER
Captain Robert Sowers in a *B-58* jet bomber, round trip from Los Angeles to New York, in 1962. Flight time: 4 hours, 42 minutes, 12 seconds. Average speed: 1,044 miles per hour.

FIRST NONSTOP
Lieutenants Oakley Kelly and John A. Macready in a Fokker *T-2 Transport* monoplane, in 1932. Flight time, from New York to San Diego: 26 hours, 50 minutes.

EARLIEST FLIGHT
Calbraith Rodgers, from New York to California, in 1911. Flight time (with many stops): 84 days. Actual flying time: 82 hours, 24 minutes.

FIRST WOMAN
Ruth Nichols, from Mineola, New York, to Burbank, California, in 1930. Flight time: 16 hours, 59 minutes, 30 seconds.

FIRST ROUND-TRIP
Lieutenant John Conroy in an *F-86A Sabre* jet in 1955. Flight time: about 11½ hours.

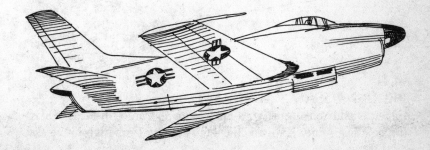

Warbirds: Fighters, Spy Planes, and Bombers

Military aircraft are classified by the jobs they do. In this section you'll learn how each one is used, all about "top gun" fighter jets, how to become a "top gun" pilot, and exciting facts about the world's most famous warplanes.

Types of Military Aircraft

BOMBERS
Also called "attack planes," bombers attack targets on land or sea. The largest bombers carry up to eight crew members, and fly long distances without refueling. The newest is the Navy's $20 million *B-1B* bomber. To date, only 100 have been built.

FIGHTERS
These supersonic jets are unbeatable in air-to-air combat and can hit ground targets as well. Usually based on aircraft carriers, they're easily recognized by their triangular-shaped "delta wings." Most fighters are armed with rockets, missiles, and bombs, carry extra fuel tanks, and can fly long distances without refueling. They are crewed by one or two people: pilot and radar intercept officer.

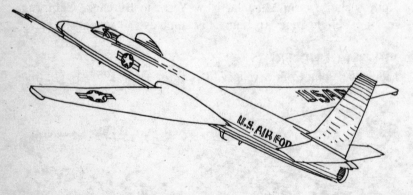

RECONNAISSANCE AIRCRAFT
Cameras and sensing devices are the major cargo on these power-ful jets. Their duty is to watch enemy activity from high in the sky.

TRANSPORTS

These enormous planes transport military troops and equipment. One of the largest is the Air Forces' *C-5 Galaxy*. The plane's gigantic nose flips open to allow tanks and other military vehicles to roll inside. In times of combat, transports are fitted with special tires so they can take off and land on rough surfaces.

TANKERS

Sometimes called "mother tankers," these planes haul large amounts of fuel in order to replenish, in-flight, the fuel tanks of other aircraft. The tank operator drops the refueling tube to the aircraft below and guides it by watching video cameras and through periscopes.

DRONES

Remotely piloted vehicles (manned from the ground), used for dangerous spy missions and sometimes as combat targets during practice flights.

How to Become a TopGun

If you saw the movie *Top Gun*, you know that only a handful of pilots make it to "fightertown," the Navy's famous Fighter Weapons School located at Naval Air Station Miramar, San Diego, California. The purpose of Top Gun is to teach pilots to perform air-to-air combat. After graduation the men return to their military bases and train other pilots. Here's how to qualify.

Be Physically Fit Pilots must be in top physical shape, of "normal" height and weight, and must have 20/20 vision *without* glasses.

Complete College Top pilots are college graduates.

Complete AVOCS Most pilots attend Aviation Officer's Candidate School (AVOCS) after completing college. There they study meteorology, engineering, aerodynamics, and learn how to become military officers.

Complete Flight School New pilots learn to fly high-performance jets and helicopters while attending several special flight schools:

    Primary flight school includes 20 weeks of ground and pilot training.

    Intermediate flight school includes 24 weeks of training in choppers and high-performance piston-engine and jet-engine aircraft.

    Advanced flight school includes one year of sea duty deployment aboard an aircraft carrier. This is where fighter pilots learn how to maneuver the jets on and off the flight deck.

TOP GUN AIRCRAFT

Here they are, the fastest fighters, bombers, and spy planes in the United States.

AIRCRAFT	TYPE	TOP SPEED
F-15 Eagle	Fighter	Mach 2.5
FB-111	Bomber	Mach 2.5

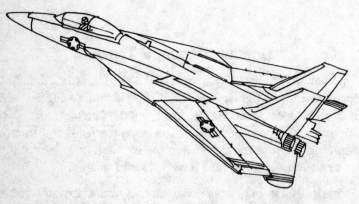

F-14 Tom Cat	Fighter	Mach 2.4
F-16 Fighting Falcon	Fighter	Mach 2.3
E2-C Hawkeye	Reconnaissance	Mach 2
F/A-18 Hornet	Fighter	Mach 2
B-1B	Bomber	Mach 1
B-52	Bomber	Mach 1

Famous Warbirds

SR-71 BLACKBIRD

Grounded in 1990, this black needle-nosed spy plane was the world's fastest (Mach 3+) and highest-flying (16+ miles) jet. Its pilot and navigator wore spacesuits. The plane's cameras could photograph a license plate from 15 miles away.

F-104A STARFIGHTER

This fighter was so fast people called it "the missile with a man in it." It was the first plane to reach a speed of Mach 2, and in 1958 it set a world altitude record by soaring 91,249 feet. It was astronaut Neil Armstrong's favorite plane.

BOEING F4B-4

A bomber in the 1930s, this biplane sped more than 176 miles per hour, and carried five 24-pound bombs under each wing and one 500-pound bomb in its belly. The machine guns fired through the arc of the propeller.

BOEING P-26A

Known as the *Pea-Shooter*, this 1930s fighter was one of the first military monoplanes in the United States. With a top speed of 247 miles per hour, it could cruise at altitudes up to 27,500 feet, hauling two 110-pound bombs and two machine guns.

CURTISS P-40 WARHAWK

The *Warhawk* is one of the most famous fighters ever built. Flown by the famous "Flying Tigers," it was known for the shark-mouth design painted on its nose. *Warhawks* destroyed hundreds of enemy aircraft during World War II.

DOUGLAS A-4C SKYHAWK

A light attack bomber, the *Skyhawk* was the Navy's first-line bomber flown during the Korean and Vietnam wars. Unlike other carrier-based fighters, it did not have fold-up wings. It set many world speed records in the 1960s.

WILDCAT, HELLCAT, AND BEARCAT

These famous carrier-based fighters destroyed thousands of enemy aircraft during World War II and were flown by America's top flying aces. In 1969 a *Bearcat* set a world record for piston-engine aircraft by flying faster than 483 miles per hour, besting a record set by a German *Messerschmitt* 30 years earlier. *Hellcats* destroyed more than 4,500 enemy aircraft during the war. The *Wildcat* is famed for its victories against the famous Japanese *Zero* between 1942 and 1944.

P-51 MUSTANG

This World War I top gun fighter flew alongside the famous *B-17* and *B-24* bombers. In 1951 airline captain Charles Blair flew a *Mustang* nonstop from New York to London, in 7 hours, 48 minutes. On the return trip he flew westbound to make the first solo crossing of the North Pole.

MESSERSCHMITT

The German *Messerschmitt* was the first turbo jet plane in combat. Designed by Willy Messerschmitt in 1935, it had a top speed of 540 mph, about 120 mph faster than the *Mustang*. The plane, which looked like a flying wing, was used by the Germans to shoot down U.S. bombers during World War II.

SPAD

Eddie Rickenbacker, America's top flying ace during World War I (1918), flew a *Spad*. The two-seat fighter was armed with twin guns, front and back, and was famed for making steep dives at

speeds ranging from 60 to 75 miles per hour. In 1916 the plane set a world record by reaching a speed of 122 miles per hour over Paris, France.

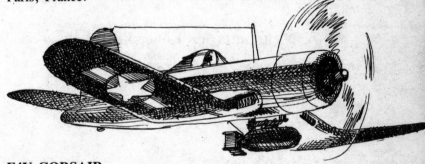

F4U CORSAIR

Nicknamed the *U-Bird*, this plane scored well in air-to-air combat during World War II and the Korean War. Its most famous pilot was flying ace Major Gregory "Pappy" Boyington, commander of the Marine's "Black Sheep Squadron." The plane carried six machine guns, extra fuel tanks, and two 1000-pound bombs under its wings. Even loaded with rockets on its wing panels, it could climb 2,890 feet per minute to a height of 8 miles.

SOPWITH CAMEL

Designed by Sir Thomas Sopwith of England, this single-seat fighter shot down Germany's legendary "Red Baron," Manfred von Richtofen, in World War I. The favorite fighter of Britain's Royal Air Force and later the U.S. Marines, *Camels* shot down 1,294 enemy aircraft during the war.

HELICOPTERS

Helicopters are rotary-wing aircraft that can take off and land vertically, hover in one place, and fly like an airplane. Military helicopters serve as attack aircraft, troop transports, and reconnaissance. Some are armed with cannons and guns while others haul equipment for antisubmarine warfare. The most powerful ones can easily lift large tanks, trucks, or airplanes with their external cargo cables. The choppers you see whirling over your city could be headed just about anywhere. They serve as passenger transport to and from airports, flying hospitals, and search and rescue aircraft. Their ability to hover at low altitudes makes them especially useful in spotting people drifting on life rafts, hikers lost in desert or mountainous regions, and traffic jams on streets and highways.

Nicknames for Helicopters

Helo   Chopper   Eggbeater   Whirlybird

Leonardo da Vinci design, c.1490

First practical helicopter flight — Focke-Achgelis — 1936 →

Chopper Trivia

- Incredibly, Sir George Cayley of England designed a steam-powered model helicopter in 1843. The chopper was lifted by four separate rotors.
- The world's first helicopter airline service began operating in 1947, in Los Angeles. Today helicopter passenger service to and from major airports is common throughout the United States.
- The giant *HH-538,* which serves the Air Force, is commonly called the *Super Jolly Green Giant.*
- The word *helicopter* comes from the Greek words *helix,* meaning "spiral," and *pteron,* meaning "wing."
- The rotor blades are shaped like the wing feathers of birds. The main rotor of a single-rotor helicopter rotates counterclockwise; on twin-rotor models, one turns clockwise and the other turns counterclockwise.
- In the early days of space flight, astronauts were rescued at sea by helicopters.
- Choppers have been known to pluck people from the rooftops of burning buildings.
- Babies are born in hospital helicopters every year.

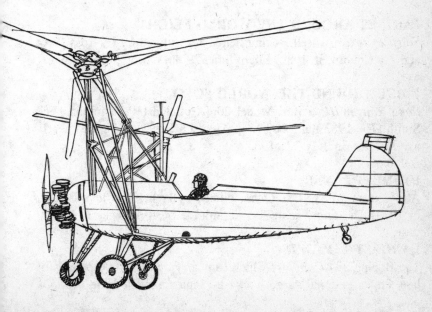

Helicopter Hall of Fame

FASTEST
The *V-22 Osprey*, which chops through the air at a top speed of 317 miles per hour and cruises at altitudes up to 25,000 feet. The $22 million *Osprey* has "tilt rotors" which can be angled for vertical takeoffs and landings or angled like the wings of airplanes.

LARGEST
Homer, a Russian-built *MIl Mi-12*, measuring 220 feet across its rotor blades and weighing 115.7 tons. This giant is almost half the size of a football field (121 feet long).

FIRST MAN-POWERED
In 1989 bicycling racer Greg McNeil pedaled *Da Vinci III* into the air, lifting it 8 inches off the ground at San Luis Obispo, California. Built by college students, the 97-pound chopper had 100-foot-long blades. In the future the students hope to win the $20,000 prize offered by the American Helicopter Society. The prize will be awarded to the first human-powered chopper to fly for 1 minute or more at an altitude of at least 3 meters.

FASTEST AROUND-THE-WORLD FLIGHT
Spirit of Texas, a Bell Boeing helicopter, piloted by H. Ross Perot and Jay Coburn, in 1982. Flight time: 29 days, 3 hours, 8 minutes.

FIRST AROUND-THE-WORLD SOLO
Long Ranger III, a Bell Model 206L, piloted by Australian Dick Smith. The 1983 flight began on August 5, 1982, and ended nearly a year later on July 22, 1983.

HIGHEST FLYER
An Alouette *SA-315-001 Lama*, piloted by Frenchman Jean Boulet, in 1972. The *Lama* soared to an altitude of 40,820 feet.

LARGEST LOGGER
The Boeing *234 Chinook*, which can carry up to 28,000 pounds of logs on its external cargo hook. In September 1988 the *Chinook*

helped douse the fires in Yellowstone National Park. It dropped more than 2 million gallons of water on the fire over a 13-day period.

FIRST LONG-RANGE CROSS-COUNTRY FLIGHT

Test pilot C. L. Morris in a *Sikorsky XR-4,* in 1941. Morris made the 761-mile journey in 5 days, 16 hours, 10 minutes, in 16 hops. The flight was tracked from the ground by a caravan of cars.

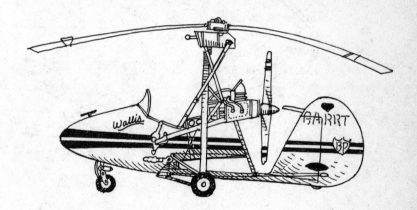

MOST FAMOUS AUTOGYRO

The *Wallis WA-116,* which has airplane propellers but no wings. Various models of this autogyro have been featured in James Bond films. British commander Kenneth H. Wallis set a world speed record in a *Wallis* by flying faster than 120 miles per hour, in 1986.

BLIMPS

Blimps are giant, sausage-shaped aircraft inflated with helium. Unlike balloons they have propellers and engines and can be steered by the pilots. Introduced in the 1800s, blimps were the first aircraft capable of flying for long periods of time. Unfortunately they were inflated with hydrogen, a lightweight gas that explodes. Nonetheless, blimp travel was popular in the early 1900s. The German-built *Graf Zeppelin*, one of the most successful passenger airships, ferried thousands of people across the ocean at speeds up to 80 miles per hour. Although modern blimps are inflated with helium, a gas that doesn't burn, people no longer travel in them. Today they serve as flying billboards and overhead platforms for photographers and television cameramen.

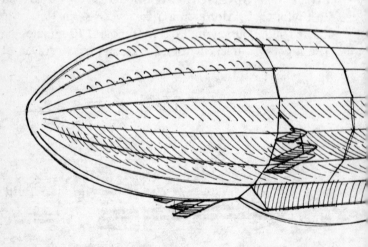

Blimp Trivia

Why are they called *blimps*? Goodyear offers this funny story. While inspecting a blimp in 1915, British commander A. D. Cunningham snapped his thumb against the airship's fabric. "Blimp," said the commander, imitating the sound his thumb had made. Afterward the huge airships were called *blimps*.

- Navy blimps patrolled the sea for submarines during World War II.
- The word *dirigible* comes from the French meaning ''steerable.''
- German Count Ferdinand von Zeppelin's first airship, the *LZ-1,* was 425 feet long and had a top speed of 17 miles per hour. Launched in 1900, it was nearly twice the size of the Goodyear Blimp.
- The difference between a *blimp* and a *dirigible* is how the airships are made. Blimps are called nonrigid because they collapse like a balloon when the helium is taken out. Dirigibles are called rigid because the outer covering is stretched over a metal frame, much like a covered wagon.

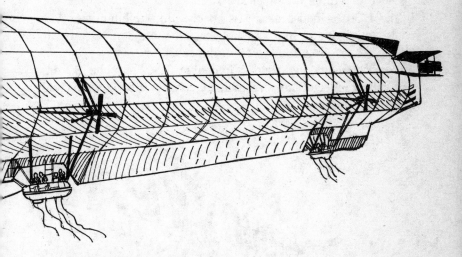

- Germany's famed *Zeppelins* served as nighttime bombers during World War I. These airships cruised at altitudes of more than 20,000 feet, higher than airplanes of the time.
- Goodyear built 168 airships for Navy use during World War II. The blimps served as overhead bodyguards to submarines and surface ships. Military blimps were grounded in the 1960s.

Flying Billboards:
Fascinating Facts About the Goodyear Blimp

Note: The Goodyear Tire & Rubber Company of Akron, Ohio, operates three blimps: *Enterprise,* based in Pompano Beach, Florida; *America,* based in Houston, Texas; and *Columbia,* based in Los Angeles, California. Each flies more than 100,000 miles a year, making appearances at major football games, car and ship races, parades, and other special events. The airships are named after famous winners of the America's Cup, a yacht race.

- The *Enterprise,* the largest blimp, is 192 feet long, 50 feet wide, and 59 feet high. It's filled with 202,700 cubic feet of helium and can carry six passengers plus a pilot at speeds up to 50 miles per hour.
- The *Enterprise*'s night sign is so enormous (105 feet long, 24.5 feet wide) that it can be read by people on the ground from a distance of 1 mile on either side.
- In the 1930s a loudspeaker was attached to one blimp so pilots could talk with people on the ground. But, says Goodyear, "people didn't like the 'voice in the sky.' "
- The "Skytacular" night sign is lighted by 7,560 red, blue, green, and yellow reflector lamps, which are connected by more than 80 miles of wiring.

- The blimps are powered by twin engines and fly at a maximum altitude of 10,000 feet. The average altitude ranges between 3,000 and 5,000 feet.
- When not in flight, the blimp's huge nose is attached to a type of cup called a *mooring mast,* which allows it to float freely in the wind.
- Blimps do not fly in rain, or in wind blowing more than 20 miles per hour.
- The maximum gross weight of the huge airships is 12,804 pounds. They can remain aloft without refueling for about 24 hours.

Messages in the Sky

Here's a list of some of the animated messages you'll see flashing on the Goodyear blimp.

- A game of table tennis
- A football player making a field goal
- Santa and his reindeer flying through the sky
- A boy lighting a Fourth of July firecracker. The firecracker explodes into an American flag.

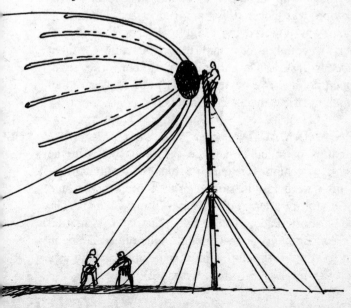

Blimp Hall of Fame

THE HINDENBURG

The largest rigid airship ever built (809 feet long) and the most famous. In 1937 the *Hindenburg* set a world record by carrying 117 passengers across the Atlantic Ocean at a cruising speed of 80 miles per hour. Unfortunately it is usually remembered for the tragic fire that destroyed it and its 35 passengers in Lakehurst, New Jersey, on May 6, 1937. No one knows how the fire started.

GRAF ZEPPELIN II

This famous German airship set several world records in the late 1920s. In 1928, piloted by Dr. Hugo Eckener, it flew a record 3,967 miles. In 1929, fully loaded with passengers, it flew around the world, making only three stops. The huge craft was 755 feet long, nearly five times the size of the Goodyear blimp, and weighed more than 230 tons.

PILGRIM

Built in the mid-1920s, *Pilgrim* was Goodyear's first commercial airship and the first blimp inflated with helium instead of hydrogen. The envelope was covered with a rubberized aluminum-coated fabric and was powered by a single engine. Carrying 40 gallons of fuel, it could glide more than 500 miles without refueling at speeds faster than 40 miles per hour. The small gondola held one pilot and two passengers. The airship was retired in 1931 after making more than 4,700 flights.

U.S.S. AKRON AND MACON

These giant airships patrolled America's coastlines between the two world wars, watching for enemy ships and submarines. Unfortunately, both were lost in storms. The *Akron* crashed into the Atlantic on a stormy afternoon in 1925, killing 72 men. The *Macon* went down in the Pacific Ocean two years later, killing all but two of the crew. Both airships were built in the famed Zeppelin Airdock at Akron, Ohio, a structure almost four times as long as a football field (1,175 feet), 325 feet wide, and 211 feet high.

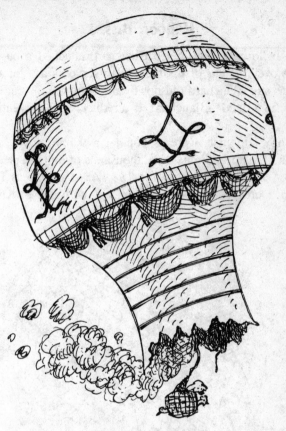

BALLOONS

The colorful hot air balloons you may have seen floating over your city are filled with heated air and are moved by the wind. Unlike blimps, balloons come in many shapes, styles, and sizes, and perform just as many duties. Scientists send them up to study air pressure, wind movements, temperature, and humidity. Many of our weather forecasts come from these balloons. People, of course, ride them for fun and sometimes race in them.

It's hard to believe that the first balloon was only 35 feet around and made of cloth and paper. Its lift was provided by smoke from burning charcoals. What's more, its "passengers" were a sheep, a duck, and a rooster, and its flight time was eight minutes.

Balloon Bits

- In 1874 balloonist Jean-Pierre Blanchard attached a huge cloth covering over the car of his balloon to serve as a "parachute." Historians say Blanchard did not fly the contraption, but sent his dogs aloft instead. Blanchard is credited with inventing the parachute.
- Pioneering balloonists were as popular as some movie stars are today. Their historic flights drew thousands of onlookers. Do you remember the cheering crowd in *The Wizard of Oz* as Dorothy and Toto boarded a balloon, hoping to float home to Kansas?

• During the Civil War (1861–1865), Thaddeus Lowe organized a balloon corps for the Union Army. The manned balloons, which were anchored to the ground with ropes, provided the soldiers with an aerial platform for observing the Confederate troops.

• Goodyear produced more than 1,000 balloons for the Americans and their allies during World War I. These unmanned balloons had steel cables suspended from the car to the ground. The cables kept enemy airplanes from flying close to the ground and thus protected the cities.

• Hot-air ballooning became a popular sport in the 1960s. Today there are hundreds of balloon clubs and associations all over the country. The United States National Hot-Air Balloon Championships are held annually in Indianola, Iowa. World championships are held in many countries every other year.

Balloon Hall of Fame

VIRGIN ATLANTIC FLYER

In 1987 this 21-story balloon completed the first transatlantic flight by flying 2,798.6 miles from Maine to Ireland, in two days.

ROSIE O'GRADY'S BALLOON OF PEACE

Pilot Joe W. Kittinger became the first person to fly solo across the Atlantic Ocean in this famous balloon. He flew a total distance of 3,535 miles, from Maine to Italy, in 1984.

DOUBLE EAGLE V

Four pilots set two world records in this balloon. They flew 5,208.67 miles, from Japan to California, in 84 hours, 31 minutes, setting the distance record in 1981. *Double Eagle V* was the first manned balloon to complete a flight across the Pacific Ocean.

SUPER CHICKEN III

The first balloon to cross the United States, in 1981. It was flown a total distance of 2,515 miles by two pilots, from California to Maine, in four days.

KITTY HAWK

Maxie Anderson and his son Kris made the world's longest overland journey in this balloon while flying across North America in 1980. Lifting off in California, they traveled 2,800 miles to Quebec in 99 hours, 54 minutes.

LEE LEWIS MEMORIAL

Air Force Captain Joe W. Kittinger set the world altitude record in this balloon by ascending 102,800 feet in 1980. He wore a spacesuit.

DOUBLE EAGLE II

The first balloon to cross the Atlantic Ocean, in 1978. The 3,233-mile flight, from Maine to France, was made in 137 hours, 6 minutes. *Double Eagle II* stood 112 feet high and was navigated with computers. A glider was also carried on board.

L'ENTREPRENANT BALLOON

This balloon was first to carry a military balloon corps. It was launched by the French Army in 1784.

CHAPTER 3

Cars, Trucks, and Monster Machines

Would you hurry to the circus just to see a car? Probably not. But in 1896 people couldn't wait to see the new "horseless carriage," a *Duryea* motorcar featured at the Barnum & Bailey Circus. Of course nobody really believed the noisy contraption would ever replace the horse. After all, everyone knew that horse-drawn buggies and wagons were the *only* way to travel around town.

Today there are more than 350 million "horseless carriages" rolling on streets and highways around the world. In America the family car is a way of life. It takes us to school, on vacations, to the mall, and just about anywhere else we'd like to go. In this chapter you'll read about the zoomy cars of the future, the most awesome sports and race cars, and even the baddest hot rods of the decade. You'll also learn about some of the nuttiest cars, and the biggest and most powerful on-road and off-road trucks ever built.

CARS

A Carload of Wacky Facts

- Spanish-speaking people laughed when the Chevrolet *Nova* was first introduced. In Spanish, *no va* means "no go."
- When a man in New York accidentally left his cellular phone in a taxi, he had no problem getting it back. He called his phone from a telephone booth, and asked the new passenger to have the driver return it.
- Henry Ford's first car, built in 1893, had no reverse gear.
- In ancient Rome, Julius Caesar passed a law banning women from driving chariots. Chariots are the ancestor of all wheeled vehicles.
- The 1990 Olds Tornado *Trofeo* came with a very smart car phone. This phone could be programmed to call its owner if someone tried to steal the car.
- Some early car tires held 60 pounds of air and had to be pumped by hand. Today the average tire holds about 32 pounds.
- In 1905 a Cadillac driver wowed the nation by driving up the steps of the Capitol building in Washington, D.C.
- In 1908 the *Model T* could be put together in just 93 minutes.

- The average speed of cars on Southern California's crowded freeways is only 35 miles per hour. That speed is expected to drop to 19 miles per hour in 2010.
- City streets in Boston were laid out to follow the trails of cattle herds.
- There were more bicycles than cars at the turn of the century. In 1897, 2 million new bikes but only 4,000 cars were built.
- Until his death in 1933, Sir Frederick Henry Royce, developer of the fabulous *Rolls-Royce,* claimed he was "just an auto mechanic." He was knighted in 1930.
- Most early cars did not have bumpers because there were not many other cars to bump into.
- In the 1980s, college student James Worden built a 360-pound solar electric car and drove 13 miles a day, back and forth to school, for four years.
- Alice Huyer Ramsey, the first woman to drive across America, navigated by following telephone poles. Her 3,800-mile trip, made in 1909, took two months.

- When "horseless carriages" got stuck in the mud, passersby often shouted, "Get a horse!"
- One early American car was named the *Jackrabbit.*
- Although the *Stanley Steamer* broke many world speed records, drivers had to stop about every 20 miles to add water to the tank.
- Artist Jim Gary found a good use for old cars. He makes skeletons of dinosaurs and dragonflies out of their parts.

Automobile Firsts

1769 The first steam-powered car was built by Nicholas Joseph Cugnot of France. It had three wheels and sped along at 3 miles per hour.

1801 The first steam-powered passenger carriage was built by Richard Trevithick of England. It carried eight riders.

1829 Sir Goldsworthy Gurney of England set a world distance record by traveling 200 miles in his steam carriage. His speed averaged 15 miles per hour.

1830 The first steam-powered ''buses'' rolled in England, carrying as many as 22 passengers.

1885 Working separately, German engineers Gottlieb Daimler and Karl Benz developed the first cars powered by gasoline engines. Daimler's gas buggy was a motorized carriage. Benz's *Motorwagen* had three wheels and looked like a giant tricycle.

1890 The first electric car was built by William Morrison of Des Moines, Iowa. Electric cars outnumbered gas-powered models until the 1920s.

1893 The first successful American gas-powered car, the *Duryea*, was built by brothers Charles and Frank Duryea.

1895 The first automobile race was held in France.

1896 Gasoline-powered cars were introduced by pioneers Henry Ford, Charles Brady King, Alexander Winton, and Ransom Eli Olds.

1897 Twins Francis and Freelan Stanley manufactured the famous *Stanley Steamer* in Massachusetts. Their *Wogglebug*, a later model, set a world record in 1906 by speeding 127 miles per hour. Their cars were popular until the 1920s.

1899 Camile Jenatzy of Belgium set a world land speed record by traveling 66 miles per hour in a bullet-shaped electric car; the steering wheel was introduced and replaced the tiller (a steering column) as the main steering mechanism.

1908 Henry Ford's first *Model T* rolled off the assembly line; Henry M. Leland, president of the Cadillac Company, changed the way cars were built by introducing interchangeable parts.

1914 Cadillac introduced the first successful V-8 engine.

1922 The first balloon tires were introduced. Before this time, tires were narrow and hard.

1948 Tubeless tires were introduced by the Goodrich Company.

1949 Ferdinand Porsche brought the Volkswagen "bug" to America. At first people didn't like the car. But by 1968 Americans were buying more than 423,000 of them a year.

1953 A Fiberglas car body was first introduced on the Chevrolet *Corvette*.

1959 The tiny Austin *Mini* debuted in England, and manufacturers around the world began building smaller cars.

1969 Japanese designers dazzled the world with the sporty *Datsun 240Z*, making Japan a world leader in car manufacturing.

1974 Congress passed a maximum speed law of 55 miles per hour to save fuel. The slower speed also reduced traffic accidents.

1976 Computer engine control was introduced by Chrysler.

1990 General Motors introduced the *Impact,* an electrically powered test car that could go from 0 to 60 miles per hour in 8 seconds, and travel 120 miles before the batteries needed recharging.

Zoomy Cars of the Future
(Road & Track *Magazine's "Top 10"*)

Scientists predict that cars will continue to be the most popular way to travel for the next ten years. And manufacturers are ready. The cars of the future will be faster, more streamlined, and come equipped with fancy gadgets and computers. Here are some of the "concept cars" that you could be driving in the future.

FORD SPLASH

This sporty car has been called a "grounded flying saucer," and the "Lunar Rover of the road." The body can be raised for bumping over dirt roads or lowered for cruising the highways. The front end has four headlights on each side.

XJ220

oxia

Cal Concept

THE JAGUAR XJ220
The body of this flashy car is built of aluminum and rides close to the ground. It's called the XJ220 because manufacturers hope it will reach speeds up to—you guessed it—220 miles per hour.

PEUGEOT OXIA
Drivers who get lost will love this car. It comes with a computerized road map that pictures the routes on screen. Computers also drive the wheels and the powerful engine.

CADILLAC SOLITAIRE
If you like your wheels covered with shiny chrome, the *Solitaire* is for you. The front end has a "windowpane grille," and under the long hood lurks a powerful race car engine. A fabulous car.

DODGE VIPER R/T-10
This sporty convertible is powered by a monster engine, and there are zoomy scoops molded into both the door panels and the hood. The oval headlights, with smaller lights inside, look like teeth. Watch for it in 1992.

GHIA VIA
Billed as the "sports car of the year 2000," this fabulous Ford has a "floating instrument panel" made of fiber optics. The headlamps also use fiber optics.

NISSAN IF
The motor on this racy two-seater is tucked behind the seats. Three features make this car special: the tinted gullwing doors (that lift up instead of out); oval, tinted headlamps; and a lightweight body (only 1,300 pounds) to increase the speed.

SBARRO DREAM CAR
Batman would love this car; the wheels look like doughnuts. Called "hubless wheels," they're bound to turn heads. The shiny rear-end spoiler is full of Swiss cheese holes. Zoom!

CHEVROLET CALIFORNIA CONCEPT CAMARO
With its slanted headlamps and sleek style, the new Camaros could leave all other cars in the dust. This model features zoomy hubcaps, and an engine that pumps out more than 200 horsepower. This one could be in showrooms soon.

PONTIAC STINGER
Huge wheels, see-through door panels, and hidden headlamps are only three of the features you'll find on this zippy two-seater. Built to cruise the highways, it has slanted front and rear windows.

Gadgets of the Future

Car telephones will be easier to use since drivers won't have to pick up the receiver. Instead, they'll push a button on the steering wheel.

Drivers who want to avoid crowded roads can use their **dashboard navigation systems,** which will tell them which streets and highways to dodge.

Radar cruise controls may be standard equipment on cars built in 2000. The controls will help highway traffic speed along at about 70 miles per hour, spaced only a few feet apart. The device will be tested in California in 1991.

Computerized dashboard maps, like *Kitt's,* of "Knightrider" television fame, may also be standard equipment in 2000. Drivers searching for the best routes will simply ask the computer to draw the map.

Space-age headlights could appear in the mid- to late 1990s. Thanks to the new, small-size lightbulb (one-half the size of a normal bulb), these headlights may be only one or two inches high. How will this change a car's front end and hood? Wait and see!

Robosaurus

What's 35 feet tall, weighs 60,000 pounds, and looks like Godzilla? It's *Robosaurus,* an electronically controlled steel dinosaur that lifts cars, flattens them in its monster jaws, and then hurls them to the ground. This flame-blowing machine often turns up at monster truck show exhibitions. Don't miss it.

The President's Car

The first presidential "car," the *Penn Coach,* was a yellow and white carriage. The governor of Pennsylvania gave it to Martha Washington as a gift, in 1787. Today the president cruises around town in a Lincoln *Continental* limousine. Known to secret service agents as *200X,* the limo stretches 22 feet long, weighs 12,000 pounds, and is covered with 2 tons of armor plating. No bullet can pierce any part of its body.

Star Cars

Many celebrities are car collectors. Here are a few of the vehicles owned by three stars.

Superstar **Eddie Murphy** has so many cars that he needs to park them on his own personal basketball court. Two of his favorites are a black Rolls-Royce and a black Ferrari *Testarossa*. When Murphy takes to the roads, his bodyguards surround his car with Mercedes-Benzes.

Jon Bon Jovi owns more vehicles than he can possibly drive. In 1989 his fleet included a 1969 Chevy *Camaro* convertible, a classic 1958 Corvette, 1988 Ferrari, 1989 Corvette, a Jeep *Wrangler,* and two motorcycles.

King of rock **Elvis Presley** owned hundreds of cars in his lifetime. His favorite, a 1971 De Tomaso *Pantera*, was sold for $2 million in 1981. But the new owner was in for a surprise; there were bullet holes in the dashboard. As the story goes, the king shot up the dashboard when the car wouldn't start.

Roadside Trivia

• The word *automobile* is a combination of the Greek word *auto,* meaning ''self'' and the French word *mobile,* meaning ''moving.'' It first appeared in France in the late 1880s.

• Americans put an average of 9,000 miles a year on their cars.

• The first parking meter appeared in Oklahoma City in 1935.

• The world's first gas station was opened in St. Louis, Missouri, in 1905.

• The highway department in California plans to put ''maintenance robots'' on the freeways by 1993. These mechanical people will work around the clock, clearing roadside litter, painting lane stripes, and sealing road cracks.

• The modern car is made up of about 10,000 separate parts.

• More than 28 million American families own more than one car.

• Motor vehicles in America consume more than 115 billion gallons of fuel every year.

• America's passenger cars travel more than 1.5 trillion miles every year.

- The average car weighs about 3,200 pounds.
- If you need a place to park, try Canada's West Edmonton Mall in Alberta. The lot can hold about 30,000 cars.
- U.S. roads going north and south are odd-numbered. Those traveling east and west are even-numbered.
- Most early ''highways'' were little more than dirt roads rutted by carriage wheels.
- Before traffic signals were introduced in 1920, police held hand-operated lights to direct traffic.
- With its 52 pumps, *Little America,* near Cheyenne, Wyoming, is thought to be the world's largest gas station.
- There are more registered drivers in the United States than in any other country, and more in California than in any other state.
- Over the years manufacturers have produced more than 10,000 makes of cars.
- The Goodyear Tire and Rubber Company manufactures what may be the world's largest truck tires. These monsters measure 11 feet in diameter, weigh 12,500 pounds, and cost $75,000 each.
- The first license plates appeared in France in 1893; the first U.S. plates appeared in New York in 1901.
- The Ford *Escort,* which debuted in 1980, was the world's best-selling car until 1988. In 1989 the honor went to the Honda *Accord*.

Cars in the Fast Lane

CAR	0-60 MPH	¼ MILE	BRAKING FROM 80 MPH
Porsche *Ruf* 3.4 Turbo	4.5 seconds	13.0 seconds	243 feet
Corvette *ZR1*	4.9 seconds	13.4 seconds	233 feet
Porsche *Carrera 4*	4.9 seconds	13.5 seconds	218 feet
Ferrari *GTO*	5.0 seconds	14.1 seconds	240 feet
Porsche *911* Turbo	5.1 seconds	13.6 seconds	239 feet

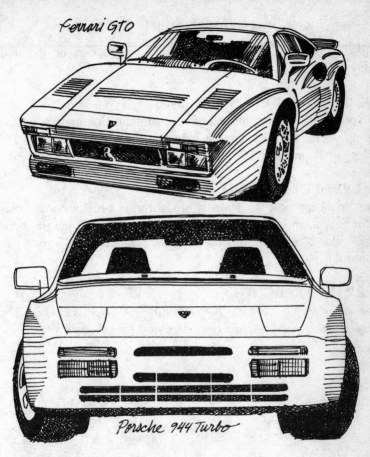

Ferrari GTO

Porsche 944 Turbo

Lamborghini *Countach*	5.2 seconds	13.7 seconds	252 feet
Lotus *Esprit* **Turbo**	5.2 seconds	13.6 seconds	255 feet
Pontiac *Trans Am* **Turbo**	5.3 seconds	13.9 seconds	269 feet
Porsche *944* **Turbo S**	5.5 seconds	14.2 seconds	232 feet
Porsche *928 S4*	5.5 seconds	13.9 seconds	234 feet

(RESULTS OF THE ROAD TEST SUMMARY CONDUCTED BY *ROAD & TRACK* MAGAZINE, 1989)

Seven Super Sports Cars

A listing of some of the most fabulous sports cars on the road today.

LAMBORGHINI COUNTACH 5000

The powerful Lamborghini features a stunning aluminum body and flip-up doors. Built by hand in Italy, it can reach speeds up to 180 miles per hour. Only 200 of these beauties are built every year.

CHEVROLET CAMARO IROC-Z

This "concept" car has already hit California's highways and may be in your town by 1993. The headlights are slanted, the front end looks like a smiling mouth, and the top features a two-part moonroof.

FERRARI TESTAROSSA

This flashy race car can reach speeds up to 180 miles per hour. The body is snazzy and the interior has every gadget imaginable.

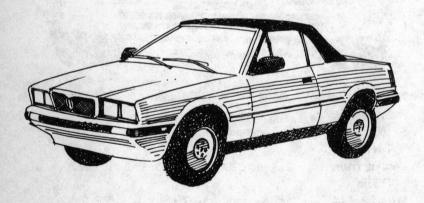

MASERATI SPYDER

The Maserati *Spyder* is as stylish as it is racy. The famous trident emblem can be found on the front and the rear ends and on the hubs of all four wheels.

LOTUS ESPRIT TURBO SE

This fabulous two-seater is a powerhouse. The turbo-charged engine sits behind the driver's seat, pushing the car to speeds faster than 160 miles per hour.

SAAB TURBO 9000

SAAB of Sweden is an aircraft company, so it's not surprising that this car darts through the air like a jet. In road races, the *9000* takes the corners like a roller coaster. Zoom!

CORVETTE ZR1

This head-turning "vette" is built like a race car. Its body is molded of Fiberglas and there's a special steel cage surrounding the driver's seat. Only 54 were built in 1990.

PORSCHE CARRERA 4

The spoiler (a device that presses the rear wheels down and helps the car hug the road) on this magnificent two-seater pops up automatically when the car reaches 50 miles per hour. It backs down when speeds drop to 7 miles per hour or less. The body features rounded front and rear fenders.

Car Talk, A to Z

Accelerator Also called the "gas pedal." The pedal controls the amount of fuel fed to the engine and thus the car's speed.

Battery Stores electrical power that operates the starter, horn, lights, radio, and other instruments.

Carburetor A device that mixes air with gasoline to burn fuel. Some late-model cars do not have carburetors. Instead, they have automatic fuel-injection systems, which feed fuel directly into the cylinders.

Coil Mechanism that steps up the amount of electricity stored in the battery to operate the spark plugs.

Crankshaft Device that transfers power from the pistons to the transmission.

Dipstick Metal device used to measure the amount of oil in the crankcase.

Distributor Distributes sparks from the coil to the spark plugs.

Exhaust Pipe that pulls spent smoke and gases out of the engine and away from the car.

Fuel Pump Draws fuel from the gas tank through a filter and on to the carburetor.

Horsepower A unit of measurement for engine power.

Muffler Device that quiets the noises produced by spent gases.

Radiator Unit that cools the water in the cooling system.

Spark Plugs Generates sparks to ignite the air-and-gas mixture in the cylinder.

Speedometer Dashboard instrument displaying the car's speed.

Transmission Transfers power from the engine to the drive wheels.

Valves Intake valves open to admit gas and air to the carburetor; exhaust valves open to exhaust exploded gases.

Water Pump Pumps water through the engine and radiator.

Mutant Motor Vehicles: Twelve that Are Famous

Each of the following vehicles has been "customized" or specially built or rebuilt by its owner. How many of these world-famous vehicles have you seen?

GHOSTBUSTERS HEARSE

This crazy car appeared in the movies *Ghostbusters I* (1984) and *Ghostbusters II* (1989). It's actually a Cadillac hearse dressed up with ghost-detecting radar scopes, flashing lights, and a computerized sign that prints different messages. One message reads, "For Hire."

BATMOBILE

The zoomiest car ever built, the *Batmobile* can travel from 0 to 60 in 3.7 seconds. Featured in the movie *Batman,* the car looks like an armadillo. Its sleek black shields surround the car when it's parked and snap open when Batman commands it with his voice. Powered by two jet engines, it also has a grenade launcher, two machine guns, and a grappling hook that shoots out of the fender. The cars (there were three) were originally 1967 Chevy *Impalas.*

GEOFFREYMOBILE

The *Geoffreymobile,* built to carry the parading Toys-Я-Us giraffes, runs on potato chip power. Kids can see the potato chips whirling around in a glass box mounted on the hood. The front headlights are painted to look like eyes, and they roll around.

MUNSTER COACH AND DRAGULA

The *Munster Coach* is the family car of TV's "The Munsters." It was built from the bodies of three *Model T* Fords. The interior, of course, is wrapped in black velvet. Munster kid Eddie has his own special seat.

Dragula, built from a real coffin, is Grandpa Munster's racing car. The flip-up "door" is a coffin lid, and the front grille looks exactly like a tombstone. The vehicle is powered by a racy Ford *Cobra* engine.

THE MUMMY MACHINE

The mummy's head on this scary-looking car features huge, rotten teeth. The gold-plated radiator looks like the tombstone of an Egyptian mummy. It was built by Jack Kampney of Roseville, Michigan.

THE AMERICAN DREAM

This Cadillac limousine has 16 wheels and is so long (60 feet) that it takes two people to drive it. Inside is a swimming pool, hot tub, waterbed, three color TVs, a video recorder, ten phones, and an eight-speaker stereo system. The flat rear section outside even has a landing pad for helicopters. The limo seats 50 people.

THE RICHSHA

This three-wheeled hot rod looks like a Japanese rickshaw, the ancient two-wheeled buggy pulled by a person. The exhaust pipes look like twisted Japanese noodles, and the taillights are real Japanese lanterns. The steering wheel is also genuine, a Samurai sword.

DICK TRACY KOP-TER ROD

This car shows up at lots of car shows, and kids love it. Built by George Barris of California, the body is a Fiberglas helicopter with rotors mounted on top. The *Kop-Ter Rod,* which cost $30,000 to build, looks great on the road, but it can't fly.

STAR WARS' SAND CRAWLER

You probably remember seeing this monster tank at the movies. It was used by the evil *Jawas* to capture R2-D2 and C-3-PO. The giant tractor treads on this tank rolled over everything in sight.

OSCAR MAYER WIENERMOBILE

If you like hot dogs, you'll love this car; it's shaped like a giant hot dog sitting in a bun. The Oscar Mayer Company owns six hand-built *Wienermobiles*. Unlike most hot dogs, this 23-foot-long frankfurter features gullwing doors, a wraparound windshield, a sunroof, and a refrigerator. Watch for it in your hometown.

THE BACKWARDS CAR

In 1930 James B. Hargis and Charles Creighton drove their 1929 *Model A* Ford round-trip, from New York to Los Angeles and back, in 42 days—without stopping the engine. As if that isn't enough, they drove the whole distance backward! Night driving was a snap because they put the headlights on the trunk. And the car had only one gear—reverse.

CINDERELLA TAXIS

The flashiest taxis ever built rolled on the streets of New York in 1910. These cabs looked like glass-covered Cinderella coaches and sat up to eight beautifully dressed passengers. The plush interiors were heated, brightly lit (so people could see the riders), and draped in fine silks and brocades. Available for hire only at night, they were built by the Universal Taxicab Service company for the Hotel Knickerbocker.

Rock-n-Roll on the Road

Cars starred in each of the following famous rock songs.

SONG	CAR(S)	SINGER
"Pink Cadillac"	Cadillac	Bruce Springsteen
"Little Red Corvette"	Corvette	Prince
"Little GTO"	Pontiac *GTO*	Ronny & the Daytonas
"Dead Man's Curve"	Jaguar *XK-E* and Corvette *Stingray*	Jan & Dean
"Maybellene"	Ford and Cadillac	Chuck Berry
"409"	Chevrolet *Impala 409*	The Beach Boys
"Fun, Fun, Fun"	Thunderbird	The Beach Boys
"Miss American Pie"	Chevrolet	Don McLean
"Surf City"	Hot rod, woody	The Beach Boys
"My Frontyard's a Junkyard"	Mercedes, Volvo, Rover, and Alfa Romeo	Robert Friedman
"Mustang Sally"	Ford *Mustang*	Wilson Pickett
"Take It Easy"	Ford truck	The Eagles

Nicknames for Cars

Betsy	Clunker	Lemon	Junker	Gas Hog
Betty	Bessie	Rattletrap	Bucket-O-Bolts	Wheels
Beamer	Woodie	Hauler	Low Rider	Vette

Five Looney Laws for Drivers in the "Old" Days

NO DRIVING WITHOUT FLAGS
Passed in the mid-1800s, Britain's Red Flag Law stated that all "horseless carriages" were to follow behind a man waving a red flag. At night, they were to follow a person carrying a red lantern. The speed limit was even funnier: 2 miles per hour in town, and 4

miles per hour in the country. When the law was repealed in 1896, Britain celebrated by holding the first Emancipation Run, a 609-mile road race. The race, still held today, is for cars built before 1918.

NO SCARING THE HORSES
In 1894 the state of Vermont passed a law stating that drivers could not drive unless someone walked ahead, warning horse-driven carriages that a horseless carriage was following.

NO DRIVING WITHOUT NOTICE
The state of Tennessee waited until the turn of the century to pass this law. One week before driving a car, motorists were required to notify carriage drivers by placing a notice in the newspaper.

NO DRIVING WITHOUT ROCKETS
Not to be outdone, the state of Nebraska passed a law in 1912 stating that nighttime motorists must give plenty of notice on country roads. Drivers had to shoot off rockets every 150 yards. In between the rockets, they had to toot their horns and fire Roman candles.

NO SITTING ON SOMEONE ELSE'S SPACE
In the 1880s, horse-drawn omnibuses were so crowded that Britain passed a law stating that each passenger was to have no more than 16 inches of seat space. Some people actually carried tape measures to make sure no one cheated!

Three Car Flops

TUCKER
In 1947 America's billboards read, "It will pay you to wait for the Tucker 48." People who waited were not disappointed, at first. The *Tucker* had many firsts: a padded dashboard, swivel seats, and three headlights, one of which turned with the front wheels. And it could speed as fast as 120 miles per hour. Alas, only 51 were built.

OCTOAUTO AND SEXTOAUTO

These many-wheeled vehicles were the brainchild of Milton O. Reeves in 1911. The *Octoauto* had eight wheels, four in front and four in back. Reeves hoped people would buy it after he raced it at the Indianapolis Speedway. No one did. The following year he built the *Sextoauto*, a car with only six wheels. Another flop.

EDSEL

People said the *Edsel*'s horseshoe-shaped grille looked like "an Oldsmobile sucking a lemon." In fact, the car appeared in thousands of cartoons and jokes in the 1950s. But Henry Ford, who named the car after his father, Edsel, had the last laugh. Today, *Edsels* in good condition are valued by collectors all over the world.

Eleven Things People Put on Their Cars

Fuzzy Dice

Air Fresheners

Sheepskin Steering-Wheel Covers

Dolls with Bobbing Heads

Curtains and Blinds

Signs, such as "Baby on Board"

Garfield-the-Cat Dolls

Curb Feelers

Musical Horns

Bumper Stickers

Sunshields

Ten Classy Classics

You won't find these "old timers" at the auto wreckers. Some, in fact, are worth more than $1 million. And the fewer that are left, the higher the price. The most expensive is the Bugatti *Royale,* which sold for $6.5 million in 1986. Only six were built and all survive today.

CAR	YEAR(S) PRODUCED	SPECIAL FEATURES
Rolls-Royce *Silver Ghost*	Early 1900s	The luxury car of British royalty; winged hood figure; top speed 63 mph.

CAR	YEAR(S) PRODUCED	SPECIAL FEATURES
Bugatti *Royale*	1920–1930	One of the largest cars ever built.
Stutz *Bearcat*	1890s–early 1900s	One of the world's first sports cars; square front end, long steering column.
Auburn "Boat-Tail" Speedster	1920s–1930s	Rounded fenders, horizontal grille; hood ornament is winged lady with swept back hair.

Duesenberg

Duesenberg S.J.	1912–1930s	Dazzling chrome, long hood; a favorite of movie stars and the rich.
Cadillac *Biarritz* **Convertible**	1959	Bullet-shaped tail fins with bullet-shaped lights; huge chrome bumpers, honeycomb grille; often seen in cartoons.
Model T (Tin Lizzie)	Early 1900s	No gearbox, three floor pedals; best-selling and cheapest car, selling for only $260 in 1923.

Cord Supercharged 812 Sedan

CAR	YEAR(S) PRODUCED	SPECIAL FEATURES
Cord *Cabriolet*	1920s–1940s	First American production car with front-wheel drive; had long "coffin-nose" hood.
Studebaker	Early 1900s–1960s	In 1950s dubbed the "new European look," with its bullet nose. Most popular U.S. car until the mid-1960s.
Citroën	1950s–1970s	Very advanced in styling and engineering; body can be lowered to only a few inches off the ground when parked.
Pontiac *GTO*	1960s	Drove like a race car and won dozens of drag races; had disappearing headlights and wipers, plus hood scoops and a monster engine.
Mustang (Original)	1961	Developed by Lee Iacocca, now head of Chrysler. Car was an instant success; horse emblem on front end.

On the Racetrack

It's hard to believe that the winner of the world's first car race zipped along at only 15 miles per hour. Held in 1895, the race was run from Paris to Bordeaux, France, and back, a total distance of 750 miles. Winner Emile Levassor drove nonstop for 48 hours. Historians say he fell asleep only once, on the return trip to Paris. Modern racers don't have time to fall asleep. They drive on road courses and specially built tracks all over the world at speeds faster than 200 miles per hour.

Bugatti 35B Grand Prix racer

For Racers Only

The organization that oversees car races worldwide is the Fédération Internationale de l'Automobile (FIA) headquartered in Paris, France. The following U.S. organizations are members of the FIA and oversee America's races.

NASCAR National Association for Stock Car Auto Racing
IMSA International Motor Sports Association
NHRA National Hot Rod Association
SCCA Sports Car Club of America
USCA United States Auto Club

Trackside Trivia

- The fastest race cars are specially built rocket-powered vehicles that compete at Bonneville Salt Flats, Utah.
- Most races are held on either road courses or oval tracks.

the first Indy winner

- Ray Hourroun, winner of the Indy 500 in 1911, sped 74.59 miles per hour in his car, the *Mormon Wasp*. Modern Indy cars reach speeds faster than 200 miles per hour.
- The dangerous curves on road-racing courses are commonly called hairpin, ess, or doglegs.
- Drag strips are paved tracks with no curves.
- The first woman to compete at the Indy 500 was Janet Gutherie, in 1977. She placed ninth in 1978.
- The term *Grand Prix* is French for "grand prize."
- Female dragster Shirley Muldowney won the Top Fuel Winston World Championship three times, in 1977, 1980, and 1982. The movie *Heart Like a Wheel* was the story of her life.
- America's first track race took place in Providence, Rhode Island, in 1896.
- The Grand Prix, held at Le Mans, France, is the oldest organized road race. It was first run in 1906.

Renault Grand Prix Replica 1907

- In 1964 the jet-powered racer *Spirit of America* went out of control at Bonneville Salt Flats and left 6-mile-long skid marks.
- The first car that was not mass produced to serve as an Indianapolis Speedway Pace car was the *Newport Dual Cowl Phaeton*. It was billed as the "Car of the Future" at the New York Auto Show in 1941.

Start Your Engines: Different Types of Race Cars

TYPE OF CAR	SPECIAL FEATURES
Indy 500 Cars	Open cockpit, no fenders, one seat, airfoils, wide tires, turbo-charged engine, front and rear wings. These cars burn methanol (methyl alcohol) instead of gasoline, and blaze from 0 to 100 mph in 4½ seconds at speeds of more than 230 mph.
Formula One	Also called "Grand Prix" cars, these snazzy racers are low to the ground, built specially for road courses, and have engines in the rear. Formula Ones are famous for slowing on turns and opening up to speeds faster than 200 mph on straightaways.
Sports-Racers	The two types are *Trans-Am* (Trans-American) and *Can-Am* (Canadian-American) cars. Although *Trans-Ams* are shaped like factory models, owners have removed certain parts to make the car lighter. *Can-Ams* feature rear-mounted engines, large rear wings, and open cockpits.
Stock Cars	Most are American cars that have been rebuilt with powerful engines. So they're much heavier than other race cars. Many are fitted with roll bar cages and have standard "stick" transmissions. Stock cars can reach speeds faster than 200 mph.
Dragsters	These cars have huge rear tires, small front tires, and long, sleek front ends. The fastest dragsters can produce 3,000 horsepower and zoom from 0 to 270 mph in less than 6 seconds. A parachute pops out to help the car stop.

Amazing Speed Records

Following are some of the world's fastest specially built cars. Speeds were set over a 1-mile-long course.

SPEED	CAR	DATE	DRIVER
638.637 mph	Budweiser *Rocket*	1979	Barrett
663.6 mph	*Thrust 2*	1983	Noble
622.407 mph	*Blue Flame*	1970	Gabelich
600.601 mph	*Spirit of America*	1965	Breedlove
536.71 mph	*Green Monster*	1964	Arfons
407.45 mph	*Spirit of America*	1963	Breedlove
394.2 mph	Railton-Mobil	1947	Cobb
357.5 mph	*Thunderbolt 1*	1938	Eyston
301.13 mph	Bluebird Special	1935	Campbell
155.046 mph	Dusenberg	1920	Milton
149.875 mph	Packard	1919	DePalma
131.724 mph	Benz	1910	Oldfield
127.659 mph	Stanley Steamer	1906	Marriott

Most Awesome Race Cars
Hot Rod *Magazine's "Best of the Decade"*

1) Buddy Ingersoll's 1984 Buick *Regal Pro Stocker,* a 278-cubic-inch turbo-charged V-6 that can speed faster than 217 miles per hour.
2) Eddie Hill's 4-Second Top Fuel Dragster, a twin-engine dragster that actually ripped the asphalt from the road.
3) Mike Ashley's 211-mile-per-hour Top Sportsman Pontiac *Trans Am*, with an awesome 615-cubic-inch big-block engine.
4) Bill Kuhlmann's 6.87-Second Top Sportsman Chevy *Beretta,* the only racer to run back-to-back 6-second passes.
5) Nissan *IMSA GTP,* earning the title, "Baddest IMSA car in history," with its awesome 1989 winning streak.
6) Don Prudhomme's Funny Car, with its 5.17-second blast, the fastest time in Funny Car history.
7) Al Teague's Bonneville Streamliner *Speed-O-Motive,* with a 393 mile-per-hour blast over Bonneville Salt Flats. The car runs on 60 percent alcohol and 40 percent nitro.

8) Juris Mindenberg's Bonneville *Corvette*, a big-block powerplant that sped at 270 miles per hour, the world's fastest gasoline-burning stock-bodied vehicle.
9) Dan and R. J. Gottlieb's 1969 *Camaro Outlaw Road Racer*, blasting past Ferraris at 200 miles per hour.
10) Bill Elliot's 1986 Winston Cup Ford *Thunderbird*, which set a NASCAR qualifying record by speeding 212 miles per hour.
11) Bob Glidden's 1987 Ford *Thunderbird Pro Stocker*, which won more races than any other car in the 1980s. It also set the NHRA legal Pro Stock speed record by speeding 191.32 miles per hour at the U.S. Nationals in 1987.

Baddest Hot Rods
(*According to* Hot Rod *Magazine*)

A hot rod is a car that has been souped up or rebuilt by its owner. The following hot rods are equally at home on the street or on the race track.

1934 Ford coupe, by Cutler

1934 Ford Coupe, rebuilt by Cole Cutler of California. Purchased in 1969 for just $20, this car sped 149.68 miles per hour in 1987 to finish the quarter mile in just 9.33 seconds.
1970 Buick GS Stage 1, rebuilt by Mark Busher of Ohio. Billed in 1984 as the "world's fastest Stage 1 racer," this car ran the quarter mile in 10.48 seconds at 125 miles per hour.

1946 Ford Club Coupe, rebuilt by Fat Jack Robinson of California. Took the quarter mile in just 9.44 seconds at 149 miles per hour.

1927 T-Roadster, rebuilt by Tom Boswell and Mendy Fry of California. Mendy (a woman), drove the quarter mile in 8.86 seconds at 146 miles per hour in 1987.

1967 Nova SS, rebuilt by Boyd Gaebel of California. Ran the quarter mile in 10.70 seconds at 127 miles per hour.

1986 Camaro, rebuilt by Mike Burroughs of Tennessee. The car sped 2.5 miles in just 1 minute, 40 seconds, in 1987.

1988 Corvette, rebuilt by Reeves Callaway and John Lingenfelter of Connecticut. Sped 254 miles per hour over a 7.5-mile oval track in 1989.

1934 Ford, by Ruchonnet

1934 Ford, rebuilt by Guy Ruchonnet of California. Ruchonnet was only 15 when he rescued this car from a chicken coop. In 1988, five years later, he sped the quarter mile in only 11½ seconds.

1982 Camaro Z/28, rebuilt by Vince Granatelli, son of famed racer Andy Granatelli. This ''family'' car blasted over Bonneville Salt Flats at 242 miles per hour in 1984.

SOURCE: *HOT ROD* MAGAZINE, 1989.

World-Famous Races

INDIANAPOLIS 500

The Indy 500 is held annually on Memorial Day at the Indianapolis Motor Speedway. The oval track is 2½ miles long and sports two 90-degree turns at each end. The winner is the first driver to complete 200 laps, a distance of 500 miles. The prize money, or *purse*, is more than $3 million. Only two drivers have taken the title four times: A. J. Foyt and Al Unser.

THE GRAND PRIX

Fifteen Grand Prix races are held throughout the year on road courses in many countries. The most famous is France's Le Mans. Grand Prix courses are known for their sharp curves, steep hills, and long straightaways. The winner is the first driver to complete the laps. The driver who earns the most points in all the races combined is awarded the World Championship title.

NASCAR RACES

More Americans attend stock car races than any other type of auto race. People love to watch the cars bump fenders while speeding 200 miles per hour or more. The tracks range in size from ⅕ mile to 2⅔ miles long. The most famous NASCAR is the Grand National. This race includes the Daytona 500, held in Daytona Beach, Florida, and the Southern 500, run at Darlington, South Carolina.

WINSTON DRAG RACING CHAMPIONSHIP

The three most important drag races in America are the U.S. National (Indiana), the Gator Nationals (Florida), and the Winternationals (California). Winners of each race earn points toward the championship title, which is awarded at the end of the season. *Drag meets* are run on *drag strips* measuring ¼ mile long. Many cars finish in 6 seconds or less at speeds faster than 200 miles per hour. Drivers compete two at a time until only the two fastest remain. The champion is the winner of the final race.

U.S. HOT ROD GRAND SLAM OF MOTORSPORTS

Monster truck racing, mud drag racing, and truck-pulling competitions are popular exhibition sports. In the truck pull, souped-up vehicles try to drag a weighted sled the length of the course. In mud drag racing, powerful trucks plow through 80-foot mud bogs, usually in 3 seconds or less. Monster truck racing features trucks with tires taller than most people. These enormous wheels run right over a line of junk cars. One of the most popular monster trucks today is *Bigfoot,* a 1989 Ford with a 557-cubic-inch engine that puts out 2,000 horsepower.

What the Flags Mean

Green: start
Black: make a pit stop
Red: stop

Checkered: finish
Yellow: no passing, caution
Blue with Yellow Stripe: give way

Race Driver Hall of Fame

Following is a partial list of the hottest racers of all time.

A. J. FOYT has earned more championship titles than any other driver. He was U.S. Auto Club National Champion seven times, and took the Indy 500 four times.

RICHARD PETTY has won the Daytona 500 six times, and the Winston Cup (NASCAR) seven times.

AL UNSER was U.S. Auto Club National champ three times, won the Indy 500 four times, and made history as the world's oldest Indy champ by winning in 1987 at nearly 58 years old.

MARIO ANDRETTI was U.S. Auto Club champ four times and won the Daytona 500, Indy 500, and the World Grand Prix.

RICK MEARS racked up the U.S. Auto Club Championship title three times and won three times at the Indy 500.

CALE YARBOROUGH is the only driver to have won the Winston Cup Championship title three years in a row. He also won four times at the Daytona 500.

DARRELL WALTRIP took the Winston Cup title four times and the Winston Cup race six times.

JUAN-MANUEL FANGIO of Argentina has claimed five World Grand Prix titles—more than any other driver.

Police Cars

Kids are usually surprised to learn that police cars are simply factory-built vehicles equipped with special gadgets. Unlike the "hot pursuit" cars featured in movies and on TV, none have rocket engines, smokescreen exhausts, roll bars, or armor plating. Following is a partial list of equipment found on many late-model patrol cars.

ENGINE
Engines are standard V-6s or V-8s, measuring from 256 to 351 cubic inches. The 302 is the most popular because it's more fuel-efficient. Transmissions and power steering have special oil coolers.

TIRES
Specially constructed "pursuit tires" are standard on some police cars. Although they look like ordinary tires, they perform better than most at speeds up to 125 miles per hour.

LIGHTS
Light bars vary from police department to police department. In California, light bars must have red and blue lenses. The red lights must be solid, glow steadily, and face forward; the blue lights flash.

Takedown lights are miniature floodlights mounted on either side of the windshield. Officers use them at night to light the inside of a suspect's car.

Brake lights operate normally, lighting when the brake pedal is pressed, but may also be switched off. Officers cruising at night can switch them off to keep from being seen.

Powerful **alley lights** are mounted on either end of the lightbar and can be operated separately. They are most useful at night when an officer is driving in poorly lit areas.

Amber lights are flashed in emergencies. They're switched on to warn drivers of accidents or disabled vehicles.

THE INTERIOR

The **radio** connects the officer to the dispatcher, who keeps everyone informed of accidents, robberies, fires, and other events. Officers may transmit or receive.

The **speedometer** looks like any other but has a certified limit of 140 miles per hour. By law, police officers must have their speedometers checked for accuracy every three months.

The **control console,** or dashboard, is equipped with special buttons that activate the lightbar, takedown, and alleylights, and the cutout switch for the brake lights.

OTHER SPECIAL FEATURES

Most police cars are equipped with special, heavy-duty shock absorbers and springs. Brakes are extra large and have "fins," which quickly cool the brakes.

SPECIAL EQUIPMENT

Flares, first-aid kits, and jumper cables—for activating dead batteries—are carried by most officers. SWAT officers may carry extra armor and shields. Primary Response Teams usually carry fingerprint kits. In some states, officers are required to wear bullet-proof vests.

Wheeling Through the Ages: Zoomy Vehicles of the Past

Sledges, the first land vehicles, were nothing more than two logs lashed together with animal skins and dragged from place to place. In time, runners were added and the vehicles were dragged by oxen, horses, and dogs. The American Indians called them *travois.* Although the wheel was invented thousands of years ago, runners are still fitted to such popular sport vehicles as sleds and snowmobiles.

Fascinating Facts About the Wheel

- The first true wheels were circular tree trunks with axle holes cut into the center. They were solid, heavy, and wobbly.
- The ancient Romans called their wheels *tympani* (Latin for "drum") because they were shaped like drums. Drum wheels were fitted to war chariots and farm carts and pulled by *onagers*, wild asses.

- The spoked wheel first appeared on chariots built by the Assyrians.
- The wooden tires on the Egyptian war chariots were lashed to the wheel with animal skins. Some had sharp blades on the axles that sliced the enemy's chariot or horse.

Hot Rods of the Past

It's true. People got just as excited about buying a horse-drawn carriage as we do today about buying a new car. Following are some of the zoomy vehicles people "drove" before motors replaced horses.

VEHICLE	DESCRIPTION
Buggy	The American buggy was all the rage in the 1800s. A lightweight carriage, it was drawn by a single horse and had a sporty, fold-down top. Fixed-top models, called *Jenny Linds*, were common in many cities.
Buckboard	These horse-drawn wagons were popular with settlers in the early 1900s. They were so named because the wagon floor was simply a wide board, and the bumpy ride bucked the driver up and down on the seat.
Carrus	This vehicle first appeared in ancient Rome. It was nothing more than a chair on wheels drawn by a matched pair of horses. It was built to show off royalty, not for "commoners."
Chariot	These open-ended vehicles were used in war, for racing, and transporting royalty. The driver stood on a platform behind a U-shaped railing and drove teams of two or four perfectly matched horses. In times of war the driver tied the reins around his waist so his hands were free to throw weapons.
Curricle	Only eighteenth-century gentlemen drove the English *curricle*. The two-wheeled cart was drawn by a team of horses and sported a fold-down top and a special leather case for holstering swords.
Gig	This one-horse cart was developed in England in the early 1800s and remained popular until late in the century. There were more than 270,000 gigs rolling on the streets of London in 1864. Also called *traps*, the two-wheelers were lightweight and less stable than the four-wheeled carriages driven by the rich. Horses often stumbled on the cobbled streets and dumped out the riders.

VEHICLE	DESCRIPTION
Litter	You may have seen these wheelless vehicles in movies about ancient peoples. They look like a fancy hospital stretcher with a house perched on top. The bottom is fitted with long poles, carried on the shoulders of four strong men. Litters were used by the Romans as early as A.D. 54 and later by the Normans. In later years the poles were laid on the backs of horses and mules.

Roman Rheda	This ox-drawn cart looked like a bathtub. In ancient Rome it served as a private carriage and sometimes a taxicab. The cart sat about six passengers and was drawn by either horses or mules. Julius Caesar is said to have traveled 95 miles a day in one of these vehicles.
Royal Coaches	Only kings and queens could afford these elaborate coaches. Like Cinderella's carriage, they were decked out with gold and silver, fine drapes, plush seats, and driven by finely dressed coachmen. Most were drawn by teams of eight or more perfectly matched horses. Britain's Queen Elizabeth still rides her royal coach through the streets of London on holidays and other special occasions.

VEHICLE   **DESCRIPTION**

Rockaway   The ancestor of the station wagon, the rockaway
                     first appeared in America in the early 1900s. This
                     four-wheeled carriage came in many body styles,
                     and had curtains that could be rolled up or down. It
                     was drawn by two horses and was popular with
                     large families.

Sedan Chair

Sedan   This wheelless vehicle looked like a tiny house. It
Chair   was carried by two strong men, one in front and one
                     in back. Sedan chairs were popular in France for
                     nearly 200 years. The most elaborate ones carried
                     Spain's royalty in the 1700s.

Shay   Sometimes called *cheers,* shays were among the
                     first American-built passenger vehicles, and were
                     popular until after the Civil War. They were drawn
                     by a single horse, sat two people, and had sporty,
                     canvas-covered tops.

Surrey   These stylish carriages had fringed tops, sat four
                     people comfortably, and were popular with young
                     and old in the 1800s. They were hitched behind a
                     team of two horses.

TRUCKS

If you love monster trucks, then you've turned to the right chapter. With more than 34 million trucks on the highways today, it's hard to believe there were only 700 in 1904. Modern trucks haul about 75 percent of all U.S. industrial products, consume more than 40 billion gallons of fuel every year, and work around the clock. Read on to learn the special language spoken by truckers; find out which trucks are the largest and carry the heaviest loads, and all about the powerful off-road monsters working in your city.

Three Types of Trucks

Trucks come in different sizes and shapes and do all kinds of jobs. Following are the three main categories of trucks.

Light trucks, the most common variety, weigh less than 10,000 pounds and haul loads weighing up to 1½ short tons (a short ton equals 2000 pounds). They include pickups, panel and tow trucks, and recreational vans. Most are powered by gasoline engines.

Medium trucks, the commercial haulers, weigh between 10,000 and 20,000 pounds. They include flatbeds, bottlers, platform trucks, multistop trucks, heavy vans, and motor homes. Most are powered by diesel engines.

Heavy trucks weigh between 20,000 and 26,000 pounds. They include log carriers, tractors and semitrailer rigs, and garbage, ready-mix (concrete), and dump trucks. Almost all are diesel-powered.

18 Must-Have Items Hauled by Trucks

Blood (bloodmobiles)
Books (bookmobiles)
Concrete
Farm machinery
Firefighting equipment
Fresh flowers and plants

Fresh fruit and vegetables
Fuel
Furniture and household goods
Garbage
Grain and seeds
Livestock

Mail
Medical equipment
Military troops
Military weapons
Road equipment
Rockets

Truck Trivia

• The first toy trucks made by the Tonka Toy manufacturing company were a steam shovel and a crane. The word *tonka* means "great" in the language of the Sioux Indians.

• Most early U.S. trucks were powered by steam or electrical engines.

1920 Ford TT Truck

- Inter-city trucking began during World War I when trucks hauled war supplies to seaports on the East coast for shipment to war zones overseas.
- Some early roads were so badly rutted that trucks often fell apart after driving only 100 miles.
- A *tandem rig* is a truck that pulls two trailers.
- The *Marion 8 Caterpillar Crawler,* which hauls Saturn V rockets to the launch pad, sports the world's largest windshield wipers: 42-inch-long blades. The average car wiper is only 9 inches long.
- In some states, tractor-trailers are commonly called *18-wheelers*. Fully loaded, these vehicles weigh as much or more than four standard cars, or about 120,000 pounds.
- *Lorry* is the British word for "truck."
- The word *truck* originally meant "to barter." Today it sometimes stands for *speed,* as in "Keep on truckin'."
- Heavy trucks have four or five times as many gears as most family cars. An 18-wheeler may have 20 gears forward and 10 for backing up. The extra gears help truckers drive in all types of weather on every imaginable type of road.

- Truck farmers are growers who raise vegetables to be sold in nearby or distant cities. The farmers work together, so their vegetables can be shipped with the goods of other farmers, therefore reducing shipping costs.

Truck Talk

The language of CB (Citizens Band) radios is used daily by thousands of truckers as well as long-distance travelers and radio operators all over the U.S. Here are some of the most colorful terms.

Bear or smokey Police
Bear trap Radar
Bone box Ambulance
Bubble trouble Tire problems
Bubblegummers Kids
Cackle crate Poultry truck
Christmas card Speeding ticket
Double nickel The 55 mph speed limit
Draggin' wagon Tow truck or wrecker
Evel Knievel Motorcycle
Gear jammer Truck driver
Haircut palace Low bridge or overpass
Hammer down Drive fast
Handle CBer's nickname
Hole in the wall Tunnel
Kiddie car School bus
Mercy! Used instead of swear words, which are illegal on the air
Motion lotion Fuel
Nap trap Motel or rest stop
Nature break Restroom stop
Padiddle Car with one headlight out
Pedal pusher Bicycle rider
Piggy bank Toll booth
Roller skate Any small car
Sleepin' peepers Car with no headlights
Toenail time Driving at maximum speed

Rolling Thunder: Off-Road Warriors

Following is a list of the world's heaviest trucks and their duties.

NAME	JOB
Combine	Cuts, threshes, and stores corn, rice, wheat, or soybeans. The heads may be changed to harvest different products.
Compactor	Compresses garbage dumped by garbage trucks. Steel-bladed "chopper wheels" crush and chop the trash while the giant bulldozer blade spreads it. Compactors are also used to smooth asphalt for road construction.
Crash Truck	Serves as a fire and rescue vehicle at airports. Built for speed, these 8-wheelers can speed up to 55 mph in 35 seconds or less. The top turret sprays up to 1600 gallons of foam per minute. Tanks are heated in winter to keep water from freezing.
Front-End Loader	Moves and dumps loads such as iron or coal. Some have buckets that can lift 66,000 pounds or more. Tires may be as high as 12 feet, cost $45,000 each, and wear out every six months. Top speed: 12 mph.
Giant Snowblower	For clearing airport runways. The largest ones can blow 50 tons of snow per minute. The blades may be as high as 7 feet. Tanks hold up to 200 gallons of fuel.
Graders	Smooths and shapes dirt that has been moved and compacted. The huge front wheels can be tipped side-to-side so the vehicle can climb steep banks or make tight turns. The monster blade can also be angled. Some graders weigh as much as 27,000 pounds.
Heavy-Equipment Carrier	Hauls giant shovels, bulldozers, and other large, heavy, slow-moving machines. Drivers load and unload the enormous flatbed by driving the vehicles up and down a ramp.

NAME	JOB
Lattic Boom	Crane that lifts cargo as high as 600 feet into the air. The largest models can hoist weights equal to seven large bulldozers. The boom, which rests on a concrete pad during operation, is transported by two 18-wheelers, otherwise known as semitrucks.
Log Stacker	For moving and stacking logs. The largest ones weigh 200,000 pounds and can lift 140,000 pounds of logs. Front wheels may be as tall as 9 feet. Top speed: 12 mph.
Mine Truck	Carries ore from mine pits to processing plants. These monster dump trucks can haul more than 160 tons of ore, about the weight of 34 full-sized elephants. Tires may be as tall as 10 feet, cost about $13,000 each, and wear out every six months.
Platform Loader	Loads large cargo onto airplanes. The long platform can be tilted from side to side or up and down, and raised as high as 13 feet while carrying 40,000 pounds or more of cargo. The cargo is moved along the platform by rollers.
Ready-Mix Truck	These rugged 8-wheelers usually carry about 28 tons of wet concrete, and nearly 400 gallons of water. Chutes can be lengthened to 20 feet or more.
Roller	Compacts soft asphalt. The huge rolling drum creates a weight of more than 27,000 pounds. Water, sprayed on the drum, keeps the roller from sticking to the dirt. Some roller drums are more than 7 feet in diameter.
Tree Crusher	Clears forests of trees and brush. The wide wheels on this vehicle look like steel barrels. Trees are pushed over by a 10-foot-high bar, and trunks are crushed by wheel blades called *grousers*. At peak speed—3½ mph—crushers can clear about 6 acres of forest per hour.

Fire Trucks

The first firefighting organization began in ancient Rome. The men patrolled the streets on foot and scouted for fires. Firefighters today are highly trained professionals. These brave men and women are trained to give medical help, to rescue people from wrecked cars and trucks, burning buildings, and clifftops, and, of course, to put out fires. The modern firefighting motto is: "You light 'em, we fight 'em."

Fascinating Facts About Firefighting

- America's first paid fire department was established in Boston, in 1679. The crews pulled and operated hand pumps.
- The first volunteer fire department was organized by Benjamin Franklin in Philadelphia, in 1736.
- In the mid-1800s, hand pumpers were finally replaced by steam-powered pumpers drawn by horses.
- Some early American roads were so badly rutted that some firefighters raced to the rescue on motorcycles. These motorcycles had sidecars (two-wheeled vehicles attached to the motorcycle) to carry equipment.
- Steam pumpers were replaced by gasoline engines in the early 1900s.
- Modern fire trucks are commonly called *rigs*.
- Some hoses weigh as much as 77 pounds fully loaded, stretch up to 250 feet long, and measure 2½ inches in diameter.
- Modern pumpers can discharge anywhere from 500 to 1,500 gallons of water per minute.

Major Types of Fire Trucks

If you've visited your neighborhood fire station, you know there are several different types of trucks. Here's how the trucks are used.

Pumpers may carry their own supply of water as well as hoses that draw water from fire hydrants. The water drawn from the hydrant is sent into the pumper and then comes into the hose at whatever rate the operator decides.

Ladder trucks come in two types: Aerial ladders, which rise up to about 100 feet, or about eight stories high; and elevating platforms, called *snorkels,* which have cage-like platforms that lift as high as 14 stories (150 feet). These trucks also carry torches for cutting metal, axes, sledgehammers, and power saws.

Rescue trucks carry emergency medical supplies; the "jaws of life"—for cutting people out of cars and shoring material for trench rescues or cave-ins; fire-resistant suits; hydraulic lifts for lifting heavy objects; and diving gear.

Hall of Flame

MOST POWERFUL PUMPER

New York City's *Super Pumper,* in service from 1965 to 1982. This rig, working together with a *Super Tender* and three satellite hose tenders, could pump 8,000 gallons of water per minute, a total of 37 tons of water. It was as large as a tractor trailer, about 44 feet long.

SPEEDIEST FIRE TRUCK

In 1982 the Jaguar XJ12 *Chubb Firefighter* was clocked at 130 miles per hour while racing to a fire.

MOST POWERFUL CRASH TRUCK

Oshkosh fire trucks, used to douse aircraft fires. These 66-ton monsters can discharge nearly 50,000 gallons of foam through their turrets in just 150 seconds.

CHAPTER 4

Trains and Locomotives

If you love trains, then you've turned to the right chapter. Did you know that trains were the fastest way to travel for more than 100 years? Kids were happy to trade their seats on covered wagons and stagecoaches for the privilege of speeding West by train. For the first time in history, Grandma's distant house was only a few hours away. What's more, toys, fresh foods, and clothing could be shipped to towns in a matter of days instead of months. Yet, for all their speed, the early trains were uncomfortable; the seats were hardwood benches, heat was provided by hot-water bottles and wood-burning stoves, and burning embers from the smokestack often drifted through the open windows and set clothing on fire. Still, trains were the first vehicles to bring America together.

Today high-speed trains transport millions of passengers and tons of freight all over the world every day. Here you'll read about the magnetic-powered railways of the future, the fastest, longest, and most powerful trains ever built, and how to talk "train" with local engineers. For a peek at early train travel, board the steam-powered monsters of the Old West and meet some of the famous outlaws who robbed them. All aboard!

RAILROADS

A Boxcar of Wacky Facts

- If the world's railroad tracks were laid end to end, they would stretch more than three times the distance from the Earth to the moon, about 800,000 miles.
- When the train they were riding broke down in 1989, a California couple rushed to the emergency phone and called out for pizza. Domino's Pizza delivered 30 minutes later.
- In 1989 a Russian man claimed he could stop moving vehicles with the power of his mind. To prove his point, he stepped onto a railroad track, bowed his head, and waited for the speeding train. The train, unable to stop in time, ran him down.
- "Jumbo's Palace Car" was a giant red and gold car built specially for Jumbo the Elephant, a circus star in the 1800s. The car had double-wide doors to let the huge pachyderm in and out. Sadly, Jumbo died in 1885 after being hit by a train.
- The click-clack sound made by passing trains is caused by rail pieces called *fishplates*.
- Some Japanese trains are so crowded that the railroad companies hire people called "pushers" to squeeze passengers into the cars.
- Tinker Toys were first displayed in a window at Grand Central Station in New York City. They caused a traffic jam.
- Some African freight trains are so long that engineers ride motor scooters while inspecting them. The scooters are carried on board.
- After two railroad officials swung and missed, the famous "golden spike" that signaled the joining of the Union Pacific and Central

Pacific railroads was hammered into place by a construction worker.
- The B & O (Baltimore and Ohio) Railroad, the first railroad to haul U.S. passengers and freight, ran horse-drawn passenger cars in 1830. It was also the first line to print a timetable, the first to pull an air-conditioned car, and the first to carry a U.S. president, Andrew Jackson.

- On its trial run in New York in 1831, the *DeWitt Clinton* pulled open-windowed passenger cars that looked exactly like stagecoaches.
- Before air brakes were invented, engineers had to throw the locomotive into reverse in order to slow it down. As the train rolled into the station, workmen would run alongside the tracks and try to hold it back.
- In the late 1800s, the Ringling Brothers' circus train hauled 20 cars. Elaborate circus wagons, used in parades, were carried on flatcars.
- The first "cowcatcher" (slanted front frame) was two pointed iron rods mounted on the front of the locomotive. Invented by Isaac Dripps of New Jersey, it actually speared the cows.

- The French have nicknamed their TGVs *The Oranges* because they're painted bright orange. *TGV* stands for *Train à Grande Vitesse,* which in French means "very fast train."
- The first monorail (single-track) line consisted of open wooden cars that hung from an overhead track and was powered by a horse-drawn pulley.

Milestones in Railroad History

1500s   The first trains were open carts on wooden wheels, pulled by horses.

1803   Richard Trevithick of England introduced the first steam locomotive. It hauled 70 passengers and 10 tons of iron a distance of 9 miles.

1825   John Stevens tested the first successful U.S. locomotive on a circular track in Hoboken, New Jersey; the world's first regularly operated steam railroad, the Stockton & Darlington, opened in England.

1830–31   The *Best Friend of Charleston* became the first successful U.S. steam locomotive; railway mail service began in South Carolina.

1851   The Erie Railroad used the first telegraphs to direct train traffic.

1859   The first sleeping car was introduced by George Pullman.

1863   The first underground railway (subway) opened in England.

1867–68   Charles Harvey built the first elevated railway in New York; refrigerated cars were introduced.

1869   The Union Pacific and Central Pacific railroads joined in Promotory, Utah, forming the world's first transcontinental railway; George Westinghouse introduced the air brake.

1872   The first electrically lighted sleeping car rolled on the New York Central Railroad. Coaches were not wired for electricity until 1882.

1893   *Locomotive 999* sped 112.5 miles per hour, the world's first train to exceed 100 miles per hour, in New York.

1904   The first American subway opened in Boston, Massachusetts.

1934   The *Burlington Zephyr*, the first diesel-powered passenger train, was put into service.

1935   Union Pacific's *City of Salina* became the first major *streamliner*. Tested in a wind tunnel, it sped 110 miles per hour.

1945   The first glass-domed observation car appeared.

1955   The world's first 200 mile-per-hour run was made by an electric locomotive in France.

1966   Japanese railroads introduced the high-speed "bullet train."

1970   Amtrak began operating all U.S. intercity passenger trains.

1981   The French TGV trains began operating in France, traveling at an average speed of 180 miles per hour.

1988   The first 300 mile-per-hour run made by a West German "Maglev" levitating train. The test train was clocked at 310 miles per hour.

1989   The *American-European Express* began service as luxury cars attached to Amtrak trains. The vintage cars cost $1 million each to restore.

Trains on the Fast Track

TYPE	COUNTRY	SPEED
TGV (Train à Grande Vitesse)	France	165–322 mph
Maglev (test train)	West Germany	312 mph
Shinkansen (bullet train)	Japan	100–145 mph
Metroliners (Amtrak)	United States	80–125 mph
Rapido	Canada	80–100 mph
Best Friend of Charleston	United States	24 mph
Tom Thumb	United States	18 mph
Stourbridge Lion	United States	10 mph

Supertrains of the Future

MAGLEV

If you like speed, then you'll love the *MAGLEV* (magnetically levitated train). This train, which has no wheels, is held above a single guide rail by a magnetic force. A test model has been clocked at 312 miles per hour. Expect to board this quiet train in 2000.

HOVERTRAINS

Like Hovercraft (water vessels), Hovertrains are lifted by a cushion of air and whoosh along quietly. A French test model sped 234 miles per hour. Hovertrains are expected to carry passengers worldwide by 2010.

MONORAILS

If you've been to Disneyland, you've probably ridden a monorail. These elevated trains run on a single guide rail above the street. Some scientists believe that electric-powered monorails will soon replace other types of public transportation in large cities because they cut down on traffic.

EUROPEAN SUPERRAIL

This new rail system will be completed in 2025. It will stretch across Europe and throughout England and Scotland. The line running from France to England will run beneath the English Channel in the new *Eurotunnel*, now under construction. The rail cars will be double deckers and carry about 120 cars and their occupants. As many as 50,000 people will ride these trains daily.

Trackside Trivia

- There are 67 underground railways in the world.
- Most U.S. locomotives are diesel-electric powered.
- The average freight train hauls about 70 cars; the longest ones pull more than 200 cars.
- Road locomotives haul passengers and freight trains; switching locomotives work in rail yards, moving cars from track to track.
- In 1990 Amtrak carried more than 21.5 million passengers.

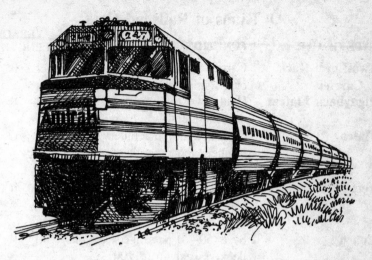

- The fastest U.S. passenger run is between Baltimore and Wilmington, a distance of 68.4 miles. Amtrak's *Metroliner* makes the trip in 40 minutes, at an average speed of 102.6 miles per hour.
- When first opened in 1959, Disneyland's (Anaheim, California) Alweg monorail had two three-car trains and was built to a scale of half the normal size. Situated in Tomorrowland, it ran at speeds of 25 miles per hour over a 1-mile track.
- In 1830 there were only three U.S. locomotives and about 23 miles of track. Today there are more than 27,000 locomotives, 24,000 miles of route tracks (between cities), and more than 187,000 miles of track nationwide.
- The speedy trains operating in Europe, Japan, and Canada offer such luxuries as hairstyling salons, gift shops, and meals served in passenger seats.
- Railroad traffic controllers are like air traffic controllers; they map train movements by watching electronic diagrams.
- Trains are kept from traveling the same tracks by the *block signal system*. In this system, each 2-mile section of track is controlled by a light signal. When the light is green, a train may enter the block. A red light means the train must wait until the track is cleared.
- Elevated railroads, called *els*, are electric trains running on tracks above the street. El travel has been popular in such cities as Chicago and New York since the late 1800s.

All Kinds of Railroad Cars

TYPE OF CAR	FUNCTION	AVERAGE LENGTH
Two-Level Rack Carrier	Carries 10 medium-size or 12 small automobiles.	94 ft.
Piggyback Flatcar	Hauls two truck trailers or containers.	92 ft.
Flatcar	Carries heavy machinery, lumber, and other items too large for boxcars.	90 ft.
Vert-A-Pac	Enclosed car that can carry about 30 automobiles, nose down.	89 ft.
Coach	Seats 50–70 passengers; double deckers seat up to 200 passengers.	80 ft.
Pullman	Sleeping car with private bedrooms.	80 ft.
Dining	Provides meals, snacks, and drinks.	65 ft.
Refrigerator	Cooled to keep perishable goods fresh; doors are airtight.	60 ft.
Covered Hopper	Covered cars that protect grains and other bulk goods from sun, rain, and snow.	54 ft.
Gondola	Can be open or covered; carries metals and bulk freight.	52½ ft.
Tank Car	Shaped like a cylinder; hauls oil and other liquids.	50 ft.
Open-top Hopper	Hauls coal and bulk freight.	44 ft.
Boxcar	Carries canned goods and bulk freight; side doors slide.	44 ft.
Stock Car	Carries livestock. Sides have open spaces so animals can breathe.	44 ft.
Caboose	Office and home-away-from-home for conductor and other railroad workers.	35 ft.

Railroad Superstars

FASTEST ELECTRIC TRAIN
The French *TGV*, which set the world's rail speed record in 1990 by traveling 322 miles per hour near Tours.

FASTEST MAGLEV
West German test train clocked at 312 miles per hour in 1988. The train runs on a 20-mile test track.

FASTEST SCHEDULED RUN
The French *TGV* zips between Paris and Le Mans, France, in just 56 minutes, averaging 186 miles per hour.

STRONGEST
The German-built *Schnabel,* which can haul more than 889 tons. Built in 1981, it runs on U.S. rails.

QUIETEST TRAIN
BART (Bay Area Rapid Transit) in San Francisco. Wheel and rail noise is deadened by rubber dampers.

LARGEST RAILWAY STATION
New York City's Grand Central Terminal, which covers about 48 acres of ground and houses 67 tracks spread over the upper and lower levels.

LONGEST SUBWAY SYSTEM
The London Underground, called the *Tube*, with 252 miles of track.

MOST SUBWAY STATIONS
The New York City Transit Authority, with 458 stations along its 237-mile route.

BUSIEST AND MOST CROWDED RAILWAYS
The Japanese National Railways, hauling more than 18 million passengers daily.

LARGEST STEAM LOCOMOTIVE

Union Pacific's *Big Boy*, built in the early 1940s. *Big Boys* hauled freight and soldiers during World War II.

FASTEST STEAM LOCOMOTIVE

The *Mallard*, which in 1925 sped 125 miles per hour, in England.

HEAVIEST TRAIN HAULED BY A SINGLE ENGINE

The *Matt H. Shay*, weighing 17,000 tons and stretching more than a mile. It ran on the Erie Railroad between 1914 and 1929.

Trains on the Fast Track

Following are some of the fastest passenger train runs in the world.

TRAIN	COUNTRY	FROM—TO	MILES	MINS.	SPEED (MPH)
TGV	France	Paris—Macon	225.7	100	135.4
Yamabiko	Japan	Morica—Sendi	106.3	50	127.6
High-speed	England	Swindon—Reading	41.5	23	108.3
Amtrak	U.S	Baltimore—Wilmington	68.4	40	102.6

TRAIN	COUNTRY	FROM—TO	MILES	MINS.	SPEED (MPH)
Inter-city	West Germany	Celle—Ueizen	32.5	19	102.6
Amtrak	U.S.	Wilmington—Baltimore	68.4	41	101.1
Amtrak	U.S.	Metro Park—Trenton	33.5	21	95.7
Amtrak	U.S.	Newark—Baltimore	56.8	36	95.7
Amtrak	U.S.	Metro Park—Princeton Jct.	23.9	15	95.6
Amtrak	U.S.	Wilmington—Baltimore	68.4	43	95.4
IC501	Italy	Milan—Bologna	135.8	86	94.7
Amtrak	U.S.	Philadelphia—Baltimore	94.2	63	89.7
High-speed	U.S.S.R.	Leningrad—Moscow	403.6	270	89.7
Talgos	Spain	Alcazar—Albacete	80.7	57	84.9
Riverina XPT	Australia	Culcairn—Wagga Wagga	47.0	35	80.6

Railroad Terms A to Z

Branch lines Rail routes not served by main lines.

Commuter train Carries passengers to and from work.

Coupler Device at either end of the car that links them together.

Crossties Wooden or concrete planks laid between rails.

Cupola Raised glass section above the roof of a caboose where brakemen or conductors are housed.

Double-heading Two locomotives pulling one train.

Hump yard Railroad classification yard where cars are coupled and switched to different tracks, usually by computerized signals.

Interchanges Rail junctions where cars are switched from track to track.

Intercity train Carries long-distance passengers from city to city.

Main-line route Rail route that links large cities.

Scanner Electric eye device placed alongside tracks that "read" the color-coded labels on the sides of freight cars. Information is reported to computers.

Shunt The act of switching cars from track to track.

Switches Pivot rails where tracks meet other tracks.

Unit train Freight train made up of cars carrying the same freight to the same place.

Railroad Oddities

LISTOWEL AND BALLYBUNION RAILWAY

This Irish railway rode on a single guide rail and rocked back and forth. Passengers and freight had to be loaded equally on both sides to keep the train from tipping over. The railway operated from 1888 to 1924 and zipped along at about 27 miles per hour.

BRENNAN GYROSCOPIC MONORAIL

Invented by Louis Brennan in 1909, this German monorail balanced on a single ground rail and was powered by high-speed gyroscopes, a kind of spinning wheel that creates a type of magnetic force. An unheard-of idea. When people worried that the vehicle would tip over, Brennan invited groups to huddle on one side while the train sped down the rails. Although he proved it worked, his monorail faded into history.

THE FLYING LADY

Built by August Belmont in 1910, this monorail rode on a single ground track that was balanced by an overhead rail. Unbelievably, it reached speeds up to 60 miles per hour while carrying passengers between Long Island City and the New Haven railroad station, a distance of about 100 miles. The line stopped flying after only three months when a car tipped over while speeding around a turn.

DADDY LONGLEGS

Everyone knows that railways run on land. Everyone, that is, but a group of British engineers who built an electric railway under the sea. *Daddy Longlegs* had four motorized "legs" attached to tracks beneath the water. Passengers rode in a round, open car mounted 8 feet above the water. What if the train accidentally fell into the sea? Lifeboats were carried just in case.

THE BOYNTON BICYCLE RAILROAD

This steam-driven flyer reached speeds as fast as 60 miles per hour. The two-story high cars ran on a single ground rail that was held in place by an overhead rail. The engineer drove the train from the upper story while the fireman busily stoked the boilers from the lower compartment. The railway operated from 1892 to 1894, in Long Island, New York.

SAIL CARS

If wind could power sailboats, why not trains? That was the idea behind the *sail car*, tested by the B & O and the Charleston and Hamburg railroads in the 1830s. The train, which looked like a sailboat on wheels, blew along the tracks at about 30 miles per hour. Passengers were less fortunate in stormy weather; strong winds blew the cars off the tracks.

HORSE-TREADMILL CARS

Imagine riding a train powered by a horse! Tested in the 1930s, *horse-treadmill cars* were powered by horses that walked a treadmill *inside* the car. The most famous car was called the *Flying Dutchman*, which zipped along at 12 miles per hour carrying 12 passengers. Riders who were in a hurry could spur on the horses.

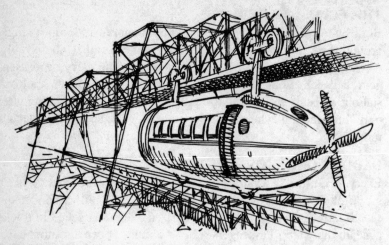

THE BENNIE RAILPLANE

Built in Scotland in the 1930s, the *Bennie Railplane* looked like a rocketship on rails; a giant, electric-powered propeller was mounted on the nose. The cars were balanced on a lower rail and hung from an upper rail that was mounted on a trestle. Although the trains reached high speeds during test runs, the commuter line was never built.

Great Train Robberies

If you ride the rails today, you probably don't worry about outlaws stopping the train and robbing you. But train robberies in the Old West were common and people feared for their lives. Bandits not only robbed the passengers but were known to derail or blow up the locomotives. Here are some of the robberies pulled off by famous outlaws of the Old West.

THE ADAIR TRAIN ROBBERY
Adair, Iowa   1873

Famed outlaws Frank and Jesse James robbed dozens of trains in the late 1800s. During the Adair holdup, the James boys derailed the huge steam locomotive and sent it into a ditch. While the terrified passengers scrambled to escape, the brothers climbed inside and robbed them.

SANTA FE'S NIGHT EXPRESS ROBBERY
Red Rock, Oklahoma   1892
The Dalton Gang robbed so many trains that railroad officials tried to trick them by sending another train ahead of the regular Santa Fe Express. The "trick" train carried nothing of value; the Express was loaded with rich passengers and money. But the Daltons weren't fooled. Hiding in the bushes, they grew suspicious when the first train stopped to take on water, sat for a while, and then steamed away. Sure enough, a second train followed. The boys stopped the train, robbed the passengers, and galloped away with the money.

THE WILCOX HOLDUP
Wilcox, Wyoming   1899
Butch Cassidy and his "Wild Bunch" robbed more than their share of trains. The Wilcox Holdup was one of the first robberies pulled off by Butch and his friend Harry Longabaugh, better known as "The Sundance Kid." On a June afternoon, Butch and Sundance stopped the Union Pacific passenger train and stole $50,000. One gang member was shot by a policeman while trying to escape. Butch and Sundance split up and galloped away on horseback.

THE CHICAGO & MINNEAPOLIS MAIL ROBBERY
Roundout, Illinois   1924
One of the most famous mail car holdups in history. The train's mail car was hauling 64 sacks of money valued at $2 million. The bandits, a postal inspector and his gang, hid in the engine cab and forced the engineer to stop the train. Once outside, they shot out the mail car windows and tossed gas bombs inside. When people jumped off the train to escape the gas, the gang held them at gunpoint. Of course, when the smoke cleared, the bandits hopped aboard and took the money. The inspector and his gang were finally caught when someone gave police an anonymous tip. All of the money was recovered.

THE APACHE LIMITED HOLDUP
Coyote Peak, Texas   1937

Teenagers Henry Loftus and Harry Donaldson thought that robbing a train would be fun, so they boarded the *Apache Limited*. Little did they know what was in store. When the conductor came by to collect tickets, Henry pulled out his gun and Harry started robbing the passengers. But Harry got scared and fired when a passenger moved toward him. During the struggle, a man grabbed the gun and pulled Henry to the floor. The gun went off as the pair wrestled and the passenger was killed. The other passengers were so outraged that they jumped the teens, beat them up, and held them until police arrived.

Whistle Signals

Most modern locomotives are equipped with air horns instead of whistles and bells, but the codes are the same. Each dot means a short toot. Each dash means a long toot.

(.)	Stop, put on the brakes.
(. .)	Answer to any signal that doesn't have an answer.
(. . .)	For trains standing at the station, back up. For moving trains, stop at the next passenger station.
(. . . -)	Protect the front of the train.
(. . . .)	Call for signals.
(- -)	Move forward, release the brakes.
(- - . -)	Approaching highway grade crossing.
(- - .)	Approaching a waiting point or a meeting for trains.
(- - -)	Approaching railroad crossing, station, or junction.
(- . . .)	Flagman go to the rear of the train and safeguard it.
(- - - -)	Flagman return from south or west.
(- - - - -)	Flagman return from north or east.

A series of short toots is your signal to get off the track!

Train Talk

Engineers and other train crew members speak their own special brand of slang. Here are some of the funny terms they use while speaking to each other.

Bad order Train part that's not working properly.
Baggage smasher Baggage person, the person who handles suitcases.
Black snake A freight train made up of coal-carrying cars.
Cannonball Fast express train, originally a freight train.
Captain Conductor.
Car catcher Brakeman.
Car knocker Car inspector.
Cherry picker Switchman.
Cornfield meet Head-on collision of two trains.
Crummy Caboose, also called the "glory wagon."
Drag A slow freight train.
Green eye All-clear signal.
Highball Signal meaning a clear track, move ahead.
Hog Shorthand for *locomotive*.
Hogshead Engineer.
Hotshot Fast freight train, sometimes called a "Redball."
Johnny O'Brien Boxcar.
Strawberry patch Back end of the caboose, which is visible at night.

Teakettle Antique locomotive.
Whistle stop Town so small that trains don't stop there regularly.
Yardpig Switching engine.

World-Famous Luxury Trains

TRANS-SIBERIA EXPRESS

This train travels the longest railroad line in the world, Russia's Trans-Siberian Railroad, a distance of 5,799 track miles. The cars' ceilings are hand-painted, the drapes made of pink silk, and the plush lounge chairs are upholstered in green. One car houses a full gymnasium while another sports a large library. Built in 1903, the train still operates today, running between Moscow and Vladivostok in the Soviet Union. The journey takes 7 days, 2 hours, to complete and makes 97 stops along the way.

THE ORIENT EXPRESS

One of the most famous trains in history, the *Orient Express* has been dubbed the "palace on wheels" and the "train of kings." Built in 1883, it is composed mostly of dining cars and coaches, and for many years ran daily between Paris and Constantinople (now Istanbul), Turkey. Spies and robbers often rode the train and held up its rich passengers. The *Orient Express* has been the setting for two famous novels, *Murder on the Orient Express* and *From Russia with Love*. Both novels were later made into movies.

THE BLUE TRAIN

Each of the 16 luxury coaches on this fabulous train has private rooms for each passenger. One famous car features a three-room suite with twin beds, a refrigerator, and a bathroom complete with tub and shower. Traveling at only 40 miles per hour, the train takes 26 hours to run from Pretoria to Cape Town, South Africa. But passengers don't board it for speed. They ride in order to be spoiled by the large crew of porters and valets.

World-Famous Railroad Tunnels

Following is a partial list of the longest railroad tunnels in the world.

LENGTH	TUNNEL	COUNTRY	DATE COMPLETED
33.5 miles	Seikan	Japan	1985
14 miles	Dai-shimizu	Japan	1979
12 miles	Simplon No. 1 and 2	Switzerland and Italy	1906 & 1922
12 miles	Kanmon	Japan	1975
11 miles	Apennine	Italy	1934
10 miles	Rokko	Japan	1972
9.1 miles	Mt. MacDonald	Canada	1989
9 miles	St. Gotthard	Switzerland	1882
9 miles	Lotschberg	Switzerland	1913
9 miles	Hokunku	Japan	1962
8 miles	Monte Cerris (Frejus)	France and Italy	1871
8 miles	Cascade	United States	1929
8 miles	Shin-Shimizu	Japan	1961
8 miles	Flathead	United States	1970
8 miles	Aki	Japan	1975
7 miles	Keijo	Japan	1970
7 miles	Lierasen	Norway	1973
6 miles	Arlberg	Austria	1884
6 miles	Moffat	United States	1928
6 miles	Shimizu	Japan	1931
6 miles	Santa Lucia	Italy	1977

Legendary Locomotives

THE GENERAL
This steam locomotive became famous during the Civil War (1861–1865) when Union soldiers captured it from the Confederacy and drove it from Georgia to Tennessee. The Confederate troops boarded another train and chased after it, finally reclaiming it as their own.

THE ROCKET
Built by Englishman George Stephenson in 1829, the *Rocket* was the first "modern" locomotive. Speeding 30 miles per hour, the train claimed a prize of $2,500 at the Rainhill locomotive trials. Interestingly, the train's name had nothing to do with its speed. Stephenson dubbed it the *Rocket* after a journalist wrote it would be safer to ride a military rocket than his train.

THE TOM THUMB
This train was so small it looked like a toy. Built by Peter Cooper of New York in 1829, it was named after a P. T. Barnum circus star who stood only 3 feet, 4 inches, high. In 1830 a stagecoach operator challenged Cooper and his train to a race. He wanted to prove that horses were faster. Hundreds of people lined the tracks to watch the horse and train run neck and neck. The *Tom Thumb* pulled ahead near the finish line and then suddenly stopped. Cooper quickly fixed the slipped belt, but not before the horse galloped to victory.

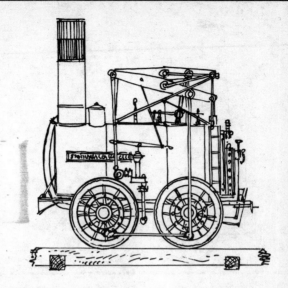

THE STOURBRIDGE LION

The first full-sized locomotive to run on American rails, the *Lion* was too heavy to run for more than a few miles. Built in England in 1829, it weighed more than 7 tons—4 tons heavier than the wooden trestles could support. But since it had been shipped from England and ferried by riverboats up the Hudson and then by canal to Pennsylvania, railroaders were anxious to see it run. Engineer Horatio Allen stoked the boiler, drove 6 miles on wooden track, and then stopped. The locomotive never ran again. It is now on display at the Smithsonian Institution in Washington, D.C.

OLD 382: THE CASEY JONES

Folk hero John Luther "Casey" Jones drove express freight trains for the Illinois Central Railroad at the turn of the century. On a foggy April night in 1900, he spotted a stalled freight train on the tracks ahead. Knowing he couldn't stop in time, he warned his fireman to jump clear and rode the train into the collision, saving the lives of passengers. When rescuers discovered his body, Casey's hands were still gripping the whistle cord and brake. People called him a hero. In memory of the event, Wallace Saunder wrote the famous verse "The Ballad of Casey Jones." Jones's home in Jackson, Tennessee, is now a railroad museum.

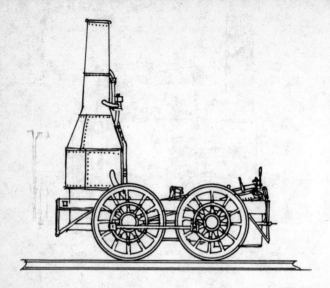

THE BEST FRIEND OF CHARLESTON

Entering service on Christmas Day 1830, this steam locomotive was first to provide regular passenger and freight service in America. Unfortunately it operated for only six months and is famed for an explosion that blew the train and its fireman off the tracks. Loaded with passengers and freight weighing more than 4 tons, it steamed out of Charleston, South Carolina. The bottle-shaped boiler, set over the rear wheels, made it look like it was traveling backward. And the racket it made was deafening. To soften the noise, the fireman tied down the boiler's safety valve and it exploded, blasting the train off the tracks.

MODEL RAILROADS

Model Trains You Can Ride

Here's your chance to ride a train just your size. "Live Steamers" are hobbyists who build miniature trains powered by real steam locomotives and run them on specially built tracks. The good news is that there are 100 Live Steam clubs in America and more than

400 worldwide. Some people are so excited by the hobby that they wear engineer's caps and bib overalls and carry old-fashioned pocket watches. The following clubs offer rides on some of the finest miniature trains in America. A must for train lovers.

CALIFORNIA
Club: Los Angeles Live Steamers
When: Every Sunday
Club: Riverside Live Steamers, Hunter Park, Iowa, and Columbia Avenues
When: Second and fourth Sunday each month

COLORADO
Club: Colorado Live Steamers (near Denver)
When: Third weekend each month, Saturday and Sunday

MARYLAND
Club: Chesapeake & Allegheny Live Steamers (Leakin Park, Baltimore)
When: Second Sunday of the month

MASSACHUSETTS
Club: Pioneer Valley Live Steamers (Southwick)
When: Sundays, weather permitting

NEW YORK
Club: Finger Lakes Live Steamers (Marengo)
When: Second and fourth Saturday, April–October

OHIO
Club: Cincinnati Cider Sniffers (Cincinnati)
When: Second Saturday each month

PENNSYLVANIA
Club: Pennsylvania Live Steamers (Rahns)
When: Fourth Sunday of the month, April–October

TENNESSEE
Club: Mid-South Live Steamers (Columbia)
When: First Saturday of the month, January–April; last Saturday of month, May–November

WISCONSIN/MINNESOTA
Club: St. Croix Railroad (across the river from St. Paul, Minnesota)
When: Last Sunday of every month, April 30–October 29

CHAPTER 5

Ships, Submarines, and Other Floating Vessels

Floating vessels are man's oldest form of transportation. In pre-historic times, we hitched rides on passing logs and drifted downstream with the currents. Today we still ride the currents—in powerboats, canoes, kayaks, Hovercraft, sail boards, and jet skis. In this chapter you'll read about the speedy submarines and hydrofoils of the future, the hottest sport boats, the most powerful warships, sunken ships, and some of the strangest seacraft ever built. Then, if you dare, climb aboard the clippers and riverboats of yesterday and meet the wicked pirates who made people walk the plank.

SHIPS AND BOATS

An Armada of Wacky Facts

- The dice game *Yahtzee* was originally called the "Yacht Game." It was created by a rich American couple for friends to play aboard their yacht. The name was changed by the E. S. Lowe Company (now Milton-Bradley) who bought the game and sold it to the world.
- The great whaling ships that sailed in the 1700s and 1800s were commonly called "blubber wagons."
- Archimedes discovered the principle of flotation in 200 B.C. while in his bath. He announced the news by running naked into the streets.

- Some historians believe the Vikings navigated by following the flights of birds. The birds, carried on deck, were released before the voyage homeward.
- *Port,* the left side of a ship, was so named because it was the side that faces the dock or port.
- *Starboard,* the right side of a ship, was originally called *steerboard* because the rudder (steering mechanism) was placed on the right side of the ship. In time the name was changed to *starboard.*
- Modern battleships are painted "haze gray" because it makes them less visible on the water. Battleships commissioned between 1888 and 1907 were painted white and known as "The Great White Fleet."

- People nicknamed Robert Fulton's *Clermont* "Fulton's Folly" because no one believed he could navigate the steamboat up the Hudson River.
- America's first ocean-going yacht was named *Cleopatra's Barge*.
- The world's longest private yacht is the 282-foot *Trump Princess* owned by billionaire Donald Trump of New York. His new yacht, to be delivered in 1992, will be 420 feet—10 feet longer than Britain's royal yacht *Britannia*.
- The crew of the *Mary Celeste* vanished a few weeks after sailing from New York Harbor in 1872. According to legend, the men were either eaten by a giant octopus or fell victim to the Bermuda Triangle, an area where many ships and planes have disappeared.
- The *Floating Palace* was a traveling circus boat that cruised the Ohio and Missouri rivers in the 1800s.
- The first compasses were magnetic needles driven into corks and floated in containers of water.
- *Packet ships,* which sailed in the early 1800s, were the first vessels to provide cabins for passengers. Before this time people rode on the open decks.
- Alexander Graham Bell built hydrofoils in the early 1900s and called them *Hydro-dromes*. In 1918 his Hydro-dome set a world record by speeding more than 60 miles per hour. The record stood until 1963.
- Lord Nelson, whose British fleet defeated Napolean's at the Battle of Trafalgar in 1815, had only one arm and one eye.
- When talking about their vessels, sailors call them *she* or *her*.

Milestones at Sea

3500 B.C.   The first known oar-powered ships were built by the Sumerians (in what is now southern Iraq) and traveled the Euphrates and Tigris rivers.

3200 B.C.   The Egyptians invented a square sail that was tall and narrow. Wide sails were not used until around 2000 B.C.

3000 B.C.   The first wooden plank boats were built by the Egyptians.

500 B.C.   The first two-masted vessels were built by the Greeks.

1000 A.D.   The Vikings sailed their long ships to Greenland and North America.

1300   The stern rudder was introduced in Europe.

1607   The *Virginia,* the first ship built in America, was launched in Maine.

1620   The Pilgrims set sail from England on the *Mayflower;* Dutchman Cornelius Drebbel built the first submarine, a boat covered with animal skins.

1776   The first war submarine was built by David Bushnell and used in the Revolutionary War. The craft did not sink any ships.

1783   The first steam-powered boat, the *Pyroscaphe,* chugged down a river in France for 15 minutes.

1787   John Fitch introduced the first workable steamboat.

1790   Iron hulls were introduced on sailing ships.

1807   Robert Fulton navigated the *Clermont,* the first commercially successful steamboat, on the Hudson River from New York City to Albany and back. The voyage took 63 hours.

1819   The steamship *Savannah* was first to cross the Atlantic Ocean. Navigators relied on sails most of the way. The voyage took 29 days.

1838   Britain's *Sirius* became the first ship to cross the Atlantic under steam power alone. The voyage took 18½ days.

1845   *Rainbow,* the first Yankee clipper, was launched.

1902   The periscope was invented by Simon Lake.

1906   The first practical hydrofoil was introduced by Enrico Forlanini of Italy. *Foils* are like stilts and lift the boat's hull above water.

1954   *Nautilus,* the world's first nuclear-powered submarine, was launched by the Navy.

1955   The first practical Hovercraft was introduced by Christopher Cockerell. Hovercraft move over the water's surface on a cushion of air.

1959   *Savannah,* the first nuclear-powered merchant ship, was launched in the United States.

1989   The cruiser *Chancellorsville* became the first Navy ship named after a Confederate victory of the Civil War.

380 Ton Vessel "Savannah"

Nautical Talk, A to Z

Aft Toward the back (stern) of the ship.

Aloft Above, on the rigging of a ship.

Amidships The center of the vessel.

Beam Width, at the ship's widest point.

Bow Front of the vessel.

Bridge Platform above the main deck where the crew steers and navigates.

Bulkheads Walls that divide the ship into compartments.

Companionway Steps leading from deck to deck.

Crow's nest Lookout platform high on the mast.

Dinghy Small sailboat without a cabin.

Displacement Weight of water, in tons, displaced by vessel. One displacement or long ton equals 2240 pounds of sea water. One short ton equals 2000 pounds. Gross tons is used as a measurement on passenger liners; each 100 cubic feet equals one (1) ton.

Funnel The smokestack.

Gangway Staircase or ramp that can be lowered from the side of the ship.

Helm The steering wheel.

Hold Area below decks where cargo is stored.

Hull The body or frame of a ship.

Lee side Side of the ship away from the wind.

Luff Leading edge of a sail; also the flapping of the sail in the wind.

Marina Special docking area for pleasure boats.

Plimsoll mark Line on the ship's hull showing how much cargo can be safely loaded.

Poop A small deck at the rear of the ship.

Port Toward the left side of the ship.

Rigging Ropes, masts, booms, and cables that rise above the deck.

Rudder Flat piece of wood or metal projecting from stern which helps guide the ship through water.

Screw Propellers located below the water level.

Starboard The right side of a ship.

Stern The back part of a ship.

Tramp Cargo vessel that operates on no particular schedule.

Tween decks The spaces above the cargo holds where extra cargo is stored.

Winward side The side of the ship from which the wind is blowing.

Vessels of the Future

AIRFISH III

Airfish III is a flarecraft, a winged boat shaped like a rocket plane that skims the water at speeds faster than 70 miles per hour. Like a Hovercraft, it flies on a cushion of air. Shipbuilders are designing the vessels in two sizes: giant, for speeding cargo across the oceans; and small, for pleasure boating on rivers and lakes. Watch for them in the 1990s.

ATLANTIS SUBMARINE FOR FAMILIES

If your family plans to visit Catalina Island, off the California coast, don't miss the new submarine tour. The 65-foot-long Atlantis submarine will cruise underwater at 3 miles per hour. From the porthole you'll see thousands of fish, brilliant-colored corals, spider crabs, barracuda, and even a few seals. The submarine rides will begin operating in 1991.

LCAC

The Navy's Landing Craft Air Cushion (LCAC) rips through the water at 40 knots (46 mph) and speeds over land as well. This amazing vehicle can climb walls, knock down trees, and carry cargo weighing up to 60 tons. Its job is to haul supplies of tanks, trucks, and soldiers from ship to shore and back.

SEAWOLF-CLASS SUBMARINES

This high-speed, nuclear-powered attack submarine will begin serving the Navy in the 1990s. It will dive deeper, move faster and more quietly, and carry more weapons than any modern submarine.

Fascinating Facts About Ships

- Most U.S. aircraft carriers are named after famous battles, presidents, or retired warships.
- Canoes, the earliest known hollow boats, date back to 8000 B.C.
- The difference between a ship and a boat is size. A ship is at least 50 feet long; a boat is less than 50 feet long.
- The Port of New Orleans in Louisiana handles more cargo than any other U.S. port.

- There are about 20 million sport boats in America.
- The world's largest fleet of public hydrofoils is in the Soviet Union.
- *Clippers*, the queens of the sea in the mid-1800s, often carried gold miners to and from California during the Gold Rush of 1848. They clipped along at about 20 knots.
- The *Spanish Armada* was a fleet of Spanish ships.
- The navigational instruments *sextant* and *chronometer* were developed in the eighteenth century.

- *East Indiamen* were large sailing ships that carried riches from the Far East to Europe in the 1600s.
- A *galleon* was a Spanish ship that carried gold and treasures.
- More ships are built in Japan than any other country; about 33 million gross tons of new shipping is built there every year.
- The Viking ships had *clinker-built* hulls, hulls constructed of overlapping planks.
- Although most modern seamen navigate with electronics, they still carry sextants, compasses, and chronometers. These instruments help them figure out exactly where they are at sea (longitude and latitude).
- The first vessel to be classified as a battleship was the *Massachusetts,* commissioned by the Navy in 1896.

Nautical Measurements

1 knot = 1 nautical mile per hour
1 league = 3 nautical miles per hour
1 fathom = 6 feet
1 nautical mile = 1.151 statute mile (1,852 meters)

Wavebusters

Following is a partial list of speed records set by vessels in all categories.

TYPE OF VESSEL	NAME	DATE	SPEED	
Hydroplane	*Spirit of Australia*	1986	345	mph
Drag Boat	*Texan*	1982	229	mph
Hovercraft	USN SES-100B	1980	103.9	mph
Destroyer	*Le Terrible*	1935	51.84	mph
Submarine	Russian Alfa-class	1983	48	mph
Powerboat	*Gentry Eagle*	1989	Crossed the Atlantic in 80 hrs., 31 mins.	
Container Ship	*Sea-Land Commerce*	1973	Crossed the Pacific in 6 days, 1 hr., 27 mins., averaging 33 knots	

Unique Vessels Around the World

TYPE OF VESSEL	SEA DUTY	COUNTRY
Balsas	Canoe built of reed bundles. Used for trading and transport.	Peru
Chinese Junk	Wide flat-bottomed boat fitted with square sail and used as a workboat and houseboat.	China
Dhow	Fishing and shipping. The ship's sails are shaped like triangles and called *lanteens*. Dhows are also called *Sambuks*.	Saudi Arabia
Donga	A shallow, covered skiff that serves as a houseboat.	Asia
Dragon Boat	Ancient paddled canoe with dragon's head on the bow. Used for transport and racing.	China
Gondola	Water taxi and tourist attraction. Poled through the canals by a standing "gondolier."	Venice, Italy
Gufa or Kufa	Pot-shaped open basket carrying people, grain, and sometimes animals. Propelled by poles.	Iraq
Hydrofoil	Speedy passenger transport that flies on foils above the water.	England, Greece, U.S., U.S.S.R.
Jangada	Fishing raft made of balsa wood. Sail is a triangle.	Brazil
Kayak	Watertight Eskimo craft, often built of sealskins.	North America

TYPE OF VESSEL	SEA DUTY	COUNTRY
Lakatoi	Coast and inland shipping and fishing. The sails are shaped like crab claws.	New Guinea
Mangrove Raft	Transport for Australian aborigines, and one of man's earliest forms of water transport. Propelled by arms and feet. Logs held together by pegs.	Australia
Outrigger Canoe	Inland ocean transport propelled by paddles. Ancestor of the double canoe.	Pacific and Indian Oceans
Pelotas	River transport. These boats are the inflated hides of pigs or cows, their feet and heads still attached, and lashed together like rafts.	Himalayas
Umiak	Eskimo's "woman's boat," for moving families and their belongings.	Greenland, North America
Sampan	Small sailboat with awnings used as a floating store, restaurant, or chicken farm.	Japan and China

Big, Bigger, Biggest

Here's a list of some of the largest vessels ever built.

LARGEST BATTLESHIP

The *U.S.S. New Jersey,* measuring 877 feet, 7 inches, long overall, about 2½ times the size of a football field. Fully loaded, she displaces 65,000 tons.

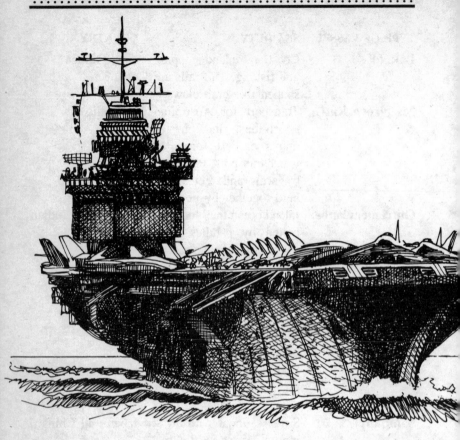

LARGEST AIRCRAFT CARRIER

The *U.S.S. Enterprise,* at 1,102 feet long. She has a full load displacement of approximately 95,000 tons, carries 100 fighters, and cruises at 35 miles per hour.

LARGEST ROLL-ON/ROLL-OFF SHIP

America's *Ponce de León.* This cargo carrier is 700 feet long and can carry more than 300 trucks or cars plus 200 40-foot-long containers. Her speed averages 30 miles per hour.

LARGEST CLIPPER

The *Great Republic,* launched in Boston in 1853. This magnificent clipper was 335 feet long and could carry more than 4,500 short tons.

LARGEST SAILING SHIP
The windjammer *Preussen*, a German vessel built in 1902. She had 47 sails, was 433 feet long and 54 feet wide, and could carry 8,000 short tons.

LARGEST OCEAN LINER EVER BUILT
The luxurious "floating hotel" *Queen Elizabeth*, destroyed by fire in 1972. She measured 1,031 feet long and weighed more than 83,000 gross tons.

LARGEST MAN-POWERED SHIP
The catamaran *Tessarakonteres*, built in Egypt around 210 B.C. Her overall length is believed to have been 420 feet, twice the size of the Navy's largest hydrofoil. She was powered by 4,000 oarsmen.

LARGEST HYDROFOIL
The Navy's *Plainview,* at 212 feet long and weighing 347 tons. Launched in 1965, she blasts along at about 57 miles per hour.

LARGEST VIKING LONGSHIP
Knut (King Canute) the Great's *Great Dragon,* built around 700. She was 300 feet long, carried about 1,000 men, and was manned by 120 oarsmen.

LARGEST FERRY
The *M/S Olympia,* which shuttles passengers between Stockholm (Sweden) and Helsinki (Finland). This giant is 581 feet long and carries up to 2,500 passengers plus about 600 cars.

Ten Hot Boats

Each of these boats had factory engines; none were rebuilt or souped-up for the annual boat test. All were timed over a quarter-mile course.

BOAT	LENGTH (FEET)	HORSEPOWER	SPEED (MPH)
Warlock	31	475	89.6
California Performance	18	575	83.7
Stoker	22	310	74.8
Magic	23	365	73.0
Shaka	20	330	71.3
Cole	20	365	70.0
Challenger	30	370 each (twin engine)	69.7
Howard	23	365	68.4
Donvee	32	365 each (twin engine)	68.1
Avenger	20	200 (outboard)	66.8

(RESULTS OF THE ANNUAL *HOT BOAT MAGAZINE* INDUSTRY BOAT TESTS, 1989)

Seven Remarkable Floaters

THE MILKY WAVE

This double-deck paddlewheeler was constructed from 40,000 half-gallon milk cartons, half of which kept her afloat. She weighed 4 tons, stretched 65 feet long, and sailed, with passengers, on Lake Winnebago in 1986.

COCONUT RAFTS

These Philippine trading rafts are constructed entirely of coconuts. Merchants pole the raft to their destinations, break off the coconuts, and sell them at markets.

ORUKTER AMPHIBOLOS

From the Greek meaning "amphibious digger," this strange steamer served as a dredge boat in Pennsylvania. Weighing 20 tons, she also had wheels for transport on land. The vessel was built in 1805 by Oliver Evans.

DEEP ROVER

This one-man submarine is constructed of 5-inch-thick clear acrylic, and can dive to depths of 3,000 feet. In 1989 she made 23 dives in Oregon's Crater Lake to help scientists study underwater activities, rock samples, and unusual plant life.

THE BURLINGTON TEAMBOAT
Animal-powered ferries were popular transport in the mid-1800s. They were powered by horses and donkeys that walked a turntable beneath the decks. The 63-foot-long *Burlington Teamboat* is believed to have provided regular transport from Burlington, Vermont, to Port Kent, across Lake Champlain. Divers discovered her wreckage in 1988.

MAYFLOWER II
In 1957 British shipbuilders built a replica of the *Mayflower,* the famous ship that carried the Pilgrims to America in 1620. Setting sail in Plymouth, England, she followed the Pilgrims' original route across the Atlantic. Fifty-four days later she arrived in Provincetown Harbor, where she is now on display.

THE ROYAL BARK OF KHUFU
Scientists unearthed this spectacular bark from the tightly sealed tomb of the Great Pyramid of Khufu (Cheopos) in Giza, Egypt, in 1954. Built to carry the pharaoh to his final resting place, she is believed to be one of the oldest vessels ever discovered. Scientists dismantled her and then put her back together for display in a specially built boat museum located near the Great Pyramid. Her 143-foot-long hull is built of cedar timbers.

Nautical Nonsense

Many modern sailors are superstitious, but early mariners were even worse. Perhaps you've heard this famous weather warning: "Red sky in the morning, sailor take warning; red sky at night, sailor's delight." While there may be some truth to that saying, there is no truth to any of the following superstitions. Ancient mariners thought it was bad luck to:

1) Get a haircut or manicure in good sailing weather.
2) Sail on Fridays.
3) Overhear a sailor sneeze while boarding the ship.

Nine Legendary Pirates

Pirates have been forcing people to walk the plank, robbing ships, terrorizing coastal cities, and smuggling stolen goods since the first vessels set sail. Even brave mariners steered clear of pirate ships bold enough to fly the skull-and-crossbones flag. Following are some of the most feared of all pirates who sailed the seas between 1500 and 1700.

WILLIAM "CAPTAIN" KIDD
Britain's King William III asked this sea captain to capture pirate ships and return the stolen treasures to England. Captain Kidd was happy to do the king's work, but turned to piracy instead; he attacked the ships and took the riches for himself. Sailing to New York, he left his treasures on Gardiner's Island. Historians say he was later caught and hanged in England. But, according to legend, his treasure is still buried on the island. The legend was the inspiration for Robert Louis Stevenson's famous novel, *Treasure Island*.

AROUJ BARBAROSSA: "REDBEARD"
This red-bearded pirate spent his life attacking Christian ships and towns in the Mediterranean in the 1500s. As commander of the Turkish Navy, he raided colonies in Spain, Italy, and France, taking thousands of Christian prisoners. He also defeated the fleet of the Spanish admiral Andrea Doria. Barbarossa's navy was finally defeated by the Christians at the Battle of Lepanto in 1571.

EDWARD TEACH: "BLACKBEARD"

The nastiest and most famous pirate of them all. Piloting *Queen Ann's Revenge* in the early 1700s, Blackbeard raided merchant ships that sailed to the West Indies and along the coasts of Virginia and North Carolina. He earned his nickname because he braided his long, black beard, and tied the ends with ribbons. Blackbeard was finally caught in 1718. His captors killed him and then put his head on a pole for everyone to see.

SIR FRANCIS DRAKE

Sir Francis Drake raided settlements around the world for Britain's Queen Elizabeth in the mid-1500s. As pilot of the Queen's flagship, *Golden Hind*, he became the first Englishman to sail around the world. When he returned to England in 1580, the queen boarded his ship and knighted him. The *Golden Hind* was displayed at England's Deptford dockyard for more than 100 years.

JEAN LAFFITE

Jean Laffite and his nasty band of smugglers terrorized Spanish and American merchant ships that traveled the Gulf of Mexico in the early 1800s. The governor of Louisiana was enraged and offered a $500 reward for his capture. The pirate laughed and offered $1,500 for the governor's head! Laffite was pardoned by President James Madison after he helped General Andrew Jackson fight the Battle of New Orleans in 1815. But soon afterward he returned to piracy. When U.S. soldiers sailed to Galveston Island to capture him, he burned down the city and escaped on his ship. No one knows for sure how he died.

COLONEL FLUGER: "OLD PLUG"

One of the most famous Mississippi River pirates in history, "Old Plug" liked to trick flatboat skippers into believing that he had been stranded. He would flag down passing boats and beg to be rescued. Then, when no one was watching, he would dig a hole in the boat's seam to make it sink. As the boat took on water, his men would come out of hiding and rob the crew, leaving them to drown. Fluger's trick backfired one day when he opened an extra large seam and the flatboat sank before his men could reach him. He drowned.

CAPTAIN GREAVES: "RED LEGS"

This Irishman became a pirate by accident, when he mistakenly boarded a pirate ship. When the pirates discovered him, he boldly challenged the captain to a duel. Greaves won the duel and the crew elected him their captain. Like Robin Hood, this pirate did not rob from the poor. After retiring from piracy in 1680, he was sent to prison, but escaped when an earthquake destroyed the building. He lived to be an old man.

SIR HENRY MORGAN

This English pirate terrorized people on land and sea. In 1671 he and his 1,400 men attacked Panama City, burning it to the ground and torturing its residents. Soon afterward he was arrested and sent to England to be hanged. But Britain's King Charles II pardoned him and made him a knight in 1674. He died a free man in 1688.

STEDE BONNET

Next to Blackbeard, Stede Bonnet was the most feared of all pirates. He forced all of his prisoners to walk the plank. Piloting his ship *Revenge*, he robbed merchant ships that sailed the coasts of South Carolina, Delaware, and Virginia in the late 1700s. Bonnet was finally captured when his ship went aground on a reef. He was hanged in Charleston, South Carolina.

Morse Code
The Alphabet of Communication

Developed by Samuel Morse, this alphabetic code is used by a ship's telegraph officers to send messages. Each dot is a short sound; each dash is a long sound. When combined, the dots and dashes form the letters of the alphabet.

A	.—	J	.———	R	.—.
B	—...	K	—.—	S	...
C	—.—.	L	.—..	T	—
D	—..	M	——	U	..—
E	.	N	—.	V	...—
F	..—.	O	———	W	.——
G	——.	P	.——.	X	—..—
H	....	Q	——.—	Y	—.——
I	..			Z	——..

AN OCEAN OF VESSELS

Following is a partial list of the world's major cargo and passenger carriers and their duties at sea.

TYPE OF SHIP	SEA DUTY
Car Ferry	Transports cars and passengers across rivers, lakes, harbors, and other small bodies of water. Some provide passenger cabins for overnight voyages.
Container Ship	Large, speedy cargo vessel that transports pre-packed goods in metal boxes called *containers*. The containers are hoisted aboard with giant cranes.
Dry Bulk Carrier	Dry goods such as grain and coal are pumped into the holds of these freighters and sucked out mechanically when the ship reaches its destination. The largest carriers haul more than 150,000 short tons of cargo.
Fireboat	Transports firefighters to shipboard fires, burning piers, and docks. These boats draw water from rivers, oceans, or lakes, and can pump an average of 10,000 gallons of water per minute.
Hovercraft	Speedy passenger boat that rides on a cushion of air. Some cruise at speeds of 75 miles per hour or faster.
Hydrofoil	Speedy passenger boat that "flies" on foils across rivers, harbors, and other bodies of water. Some average 85 miles per hour.
Icebreaker	Carves pathways through ice so other large ships may pass. The sloped bow rides on the ice, and crushes it with its weight.
LASH Ship	These freighters carry cargo-filled barges called *lighters*. The lighters are unloaded at ports and towed to their final destinations by local ships.
Lightship	Floating lighthouses anchored in areas where lighthouses cannot be built.

TYPE OF SHIP	SEA DUTY
Ocean Liner	The floating hotels of the seas, transporting vacationers to ports around the world.
Roll-On/ Roll-Off	A cargo vessel that hauls wheeled vehicles (cars, trucks, buses, etc.) around the world.
Tanker	Usually called *supertankers*, these sea giants haul oil and other liquids around the world. Some are as long as 1,300 feet, 200 feet wide, and cruise at 20 miles per hour.
Tugboat	Small but powerful, these sturdy boats guide large ships in and out of the harbor.

Unsinkable Ships that Sank

Each of the following ships claimed to be unsinkable. But, you guessed it—all of them sank.

S.S. TITANIC

One of the most luxurious and famous ocean liners of all time. On her maiden voyage in 1912, the *Titanic* hit an iceberg and sank within 2½ hours. Nearly half of her 2,277 passengers went down with the ship. Scientists located her wreckage in 1985, 2½ miles under water. Assisted by *Argo,* an unmanned deep search craft, they photographed and videotaped her remains. Today she is at rest on the sea floor.

BISMARK

Like the *Titanic,* this "unsinkable" German warship sank on her maiden voyage. First launched in 1939, she was considered the largest and most powerful warship in the world. But during her first mission in 1941, she was attacked by British warships and sank in the North Atlantic. Only 115 of her 2,220 crew members survived. One survivor, Baron Mullenheim, wrote a book about his experience. Explorers located her remains in 1989, 3 miles down.

LUSITANIA

Launched in 1907, this British liner was one of the largest
passenger ships ever built—790 feet long—and cruised at 30 miles
per hour. On May 7, 1915, the *Lusitania* was torpedoed by
German submarines and sank within 20 minutes; of 1,906 passengers, 1,198 went down with her. At the time America was not yet
involved in World War I, and protested the sinking to the German
government.

NUESTRA SENORA DE ATOCHA

One of the richest Spanish galleons ever to sail, the *Atocha* sank in a hurricane off Key West, Florida, in 1622. Her enormous cargo of gold and silver bars sank with her. Over the years dozens of treasure hunters have died searching for her remains. Finally in 1985, after searching for 16 years, American Mel Fisher located the ship, and claimed her riches.

VASA

This seventeenth-century warship sank on her maiden voyage in 1628 only a mile from her port in Stockholm, Sweden. Scientists believe she was too heavily armed and simply keeled over. In 1956, 328 years later, the *Vasa* was discovered by a team of Swedish explorers. The explorers towed her to shallow waters and brought her to the surface. Incredibly, she was able to float. Today she is on display in Stockholm harbor.

Five Famous Voyages

YEAR	VOYAGE
1492	Christopher Columbus sailed from Portugal with his ships the *Niña, Pinta,* and the *Santa Maria,* in search of the Indies. Six months later he landed at San Salvador in the Bahamas.
1497–1498	Vasco da Gama of Portugal and his four ships were first to sail around the Cape of Good Hope to India. The voyage ended nine months later, in Calicut.
1768	Captain James Cook, a British navigator, made three famous voyages to the South Pacific, and mapped the areas for future sailors. During his first three-year voyage, he sailed around Cape Horn (South America), and crossed the Pacific Ocean to New Zealand. In 1772, he sailed the Antarctic Circle and discovered the island of South Georgia. During his third voyage (1776–1779), he sailed eastward around the Cape of Good Hope, reached New Zealand, and sailed across the Pacific Ocean to discover Hawaii.

| 1831 | Charles Darwin set sail on H.M.S. *Beagle* to study the plants and animals of South America and the islands of the Pacific. At the end of his five-year voyage, he wrote his famous book, *On the Origin of Species* (1859). |
| 1947 | Norwegian Thor Heyerdahl sailed his balsa-wood raft *Kon-Tiki* 4,300 miles across the South Pacific and proved that the Polynesians were descendants of the Indians of South America. In 1950 he wrote a book about his journey, named in honor of his raft. |

Setting Sail: Major Types of Sails

Most sailing ships are rigged with more than one type of sail. The major types of sails include:

Main	Three-cornered sail attached to main mast and boom
Jib	Tall, narrow triangle attached to cables
Mizzen	Three-cornered sail attached to second mast
Forestay	Three-cornered sail attached to cables and loose

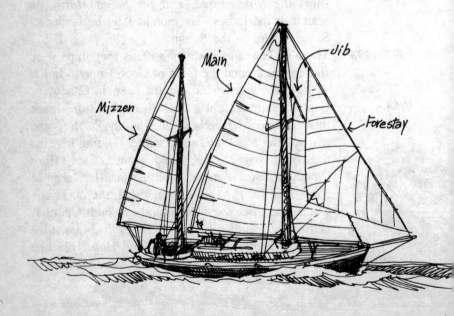

Four Famous Races

AMERICA'S CUP

This famous race has been held every three to four years since 1851. It began when the New York Yacht Club entered the *America,* a schooner, in an English yacht race and won. The silver trophy, which has been with the club for more than 100 years, is awarded to the country whose yacht wins two out of three races. It was last won in 1987 by America's *Stars & Stripes,* a catamaran, skippered by Dennis Connor of San Diego, California.

SINGLE-HANDED TRANSATLANTIC RACE

Held every four years since 1960, this race is open all types of boats. The only rule is that the boat must be skippered alone. The race extends 3,000 miles, from Plymouth, England, to Newport, Rhode Island. The fastest crossing was achieved in 1972 by a Frenchman who completed the journey in 21 days.

ROUND-THE-WORLD RACE

This round-the-clock ocean race has been held annually since 1973. Yacht skippers and their crews are allowed only three stops—in Australia, New Zealand, and Brazil. The race covers a distance of 28,000 miles, and begins and ends in Portsmouth, England.

TALL SHIPS RACE

This race was first held in 1976 to celebrate America's bicentennial anniversary. The magnificent vintage ships sailed from Plymouth, England, to New York City, and circled the Statue of Liberty. Today, tall ship races are run annually in many areas of the country.

Ten Famous Ships

NIÑA, PINTA, AND SANTA MARIA

On August 3, 1492, Christopher Columbus sailed from Spain on his flagship the *Santa Maria,* accompanied by the smaller *Pinta* and *Niña* and 88 men. On October 12, the men discovered San Salvador in the New World. The *Santa Maria* was lost on Christmas Eve that same year when she went aground on a reef, her seams split open. Historians believe the accident was caused by a young boy who was at the helm when the pilot fell asleep. The ship's wood was used to build a fort on the island of Haiti. Columbus and his men journeyed back to Spain on the *Pinta* and the *Niña*.

SEA WITCH

This beautiful clipper was painted black. Superstitious people feared her name and color and warned her captain that it was doomed. Nonetheless, Captain Robert H. Waterman sailed her from Hong Kong to New York in 74 days, 14 hours, setting a world sailing record in 1849.

FLYING CLOUD

Known as the "Queen of the Clippers," the *Flying Cloud* set a speed record on her maiden voyage in 1851. Sailing from New York, she rounded Cape Horn (the southern tip of South America) and docked in San Francisco, California, after journeying 89 days, 21 hours. Her speed averaged 8 knots. Built in America, she was 235 feet long.

THE QUEEN MARY

One of the largest and most luxurious passenger liners ever built, the *Queen Mary* ferried more than 2,000 passengers back and forth across the Atlantic for many years. During World War II she served Britain's army as a troopship. Today she is docked at Long Beach Harbor, California, and serves as a floating museum and hotel.

NORMANDIE

This French luxury liner was three times longer than a football field (1,000 feet), and could cross the Atlantic in just four days. She was famous for her elegant ballrooms, restaurants, theaters, and libraries. The *Normandie* was destroyed by fire in 1942 while docked in New York harbor.

SAVANNAH

Launched in 1959, the *Savannah* was the first nuclear-powered surface ship. Built as a merchant vessel at a cost of $40 million, she visited more than 40 ports around the world, traveling a total distance of 130,000 miles. She was retired in 1971.

H.M.S. BOUNTY

Sailing under the English flag in 1798, the *Bounty* is famous for the mutiny led by its first mate, Fletcher Christian. The ship was traveling to the South Pacific to collect breadfruit trees to transplant in English colonies in the West Indies. She was piloted by Captain William Bligh, an evil man who was cruel to his crew. Mutineers set Bligh and 18 of his men adrift in an open boat. Bligh's boat reached the East Indies after sailing nearly 4,000 miles. Christian and his men sailed to Pitcairn Island in the South Pacific, where they stripped and burned the ship. Part of the wreckage was discovered in 1957 by Luis Marden.

QUEEN ELIZABETH II

This famous British luxury liner cruised around the world for 96 days in 1986. Passengers paid thousands of dollars for the privilege. The magnificent *QE II* is 963 feet long and weighs more than 67,000 gross tons.

Buoys

Buoys are the road signs of the sea. They're marked on navigational charts so sailors can watch for them during their voyages. Some buoys have bells, whistles, or horns.

Major Types of U.S. Buoys

Nuns are red, shaped like cones, and marked with even numbers. Red buoys are placed on the right side of the harbor channel when entering.

Cans are black or green, shaped like cylinders, and marked with odd numbers. Green buoys mark the left-hand side of the harbor channel when entering.

Midchannel buoys are colored red and white, and are lit with white lights.

Buoys to Watch For: What They Mean

BUOY	WHAT IT MEANS
Green, can-shaped	Left hand-limits of harbor channel
Red, can-shaped	Right-hand limits of harbor channel
Green can-shaped with red stripe and green light (junction buoy)	Preferred channel to starboard
Red can-shaped with green stripe and red light (junction buoy)	Preferred channel to port
White with orange diamond, can-shaped	Warning, take notice. Could be site of wreck, speed limit, etc.
White, round	Anchor buoy for vessels

Horn Signals

Sailors keep their ears open for horn signals from other vessels. Look at the meanings of each signal and you'll see why.

NUMBER OF BLASTS	WHAT IT MEANS
One short	Turning to starboard (right)
One long	Leaving the dock
Two short	Turning to port (left)
Three short	Engines are going astern (toward back)
Five short	Danger, watch out
Five-second bell (in fog)	Anchored boat

Memorable Warships

U.S.S. ARIZONA
The Japanese bombing of this famous battleship at Pearl Harbor on December 7, 1941, brought America into World War II. Blown out of the water, she sank in 9 minutes, taking her crew of 1,777 men down with her. Today she rests in 38 feet of water at the bottom of Battleship Row in Honolulu, Hawaii.

U.S.S. NEW JERSEY
Commissioned in 1943, the *New Jersey* is the largest battleship afloat, with an overall length of 887 feet, 7 inches, just 4 inches longer than her sister ships the *Iowa*, the *Missouri*, and the *Wisconsin*. She saw action during three wars: World War II, the Korean War, and the Vietnam War.

U.S.S. MISSOURI

Commissioned in 1944, this battleship joined America's fleet in 1945. Aboard her on September 2, 1945, Admiral Chester W. Nimitz signed the Japanese surrender agreement ending World War II.

U.S.S. FORRESTAL

Commissioned in 1952, the *Forrestal* was the first of the large supercarriers. At nearly ⅕-mile-long (1,039 feet), she weighed 79,250 tons, carried a crew of 4,200 men, and had a 259-foot-wide flight deck. She was named in honor of James V. Forrestal, the first Secretary of Defense.

CONSTITUTION

Better known as "Old Ironsides," this Navy frigate now rests in the Boston Navy Yard in Massachusetts. Although her hull is made of oak, she earned her nickname during the War of 1812 when people said cannonballs boomeranged off her sides. In 1927 American children raised money to have her rebuilt. She was dry-docked in 1934 after visiting ports nationwide, a journey totaling 22,000 miles.

THE MONITOR AND THE MERRIMAC

These famous steam-powered ships battled for four hours during the Civil War. The *Merrimac* was a Union Navy ship taken over and rebuilt by the Confederates. The Confederates covered her wooden hull with iron plating, armed her with guns, and renamed her the *Virginia*. In 1862 she steamed into Chesapeake Bay to block Northern warships and sank the *Cumberland,* a Union frigate. Union sailors retaliated with the *Monitor,* another ironclad ship. Due to the armor plating, neither ship was damaged during the battle. Unfortunately, both ships were lost later that year; the *Monitor* in a storm, and the *Merrimac* destroyed by the Confederates to keep her from being taken over by the Union.

Ironclad "Monitor"

Four Famous Lighthouses

Lighthouses have been guiding sailors for centuries. Their bright lights shine from buildings erected on clifftops, sandbars, floating ships, and tall city buildings.

THE LITTLE RED LIGHTHOUSE

This famous lighthouse has been a child's playground for more than 100 years. It stands below the George Washington Bridge on the Hudson River. When the bridge was completed in 1931, the Coast Guard planned to sell the lighthouse. But the children of New York protested, and the building was donated to the city's Parks and Recreation Department.

PHAROS OF ALEXANDRIA

This lighthouse was considered one of the Seven Wonders of the Ancient World when it was erected in the harbor of Alexandria in the third century B.C. The tower stood 600 feet high, was decorated with marble, and took more than 20 years to build. The open fires in the tower guided seafarers for more than a thousand years. It was destroyed by an earthquake.

THE EDDYSTONE LIGHT

England's famous Eddystone Light has been rebuilt four times since it was first erected in 1698. It stands on an underwater rock ledge in the stormy waters of the English Channel.

THE BOSTON LIGHT

This was America's first lighthouse, built on Little Brewster Island in Boston Harbor in 1716. Ironically, its first keeper and his family drowned when their boat capsized in a storm as they made their way toward the lighthouse.

Sunken Ships—Ghosts of the Deep

THE KRONAN
This powerful Swedish warship sank in the Battle of Oland in 1676, taking all but 41 of her crew with her. Divers discovered her remains 90 feet down in the Baltic Sea in 1980. Her treasures included gold coins, breast plates, and a notebook. She is now on display in the Kalmar County Museum in Sweden.

THE MARY ROSE
As Britain's King Henry VIII watched from the shoreline, this galleon warship tipped over and sank in the English Channel. Built to carry 415 men, she was carrying a crew of more than 715. Divers discovered her wreckage on a seabed of thick mud in 1982. Food, preserved by the mud, was still on board.

THE CENTRAL AMERICA
Struck by a hurricane in 1857, this steamship was carrying gold miners and 2½ tons of gold and new coins from San Francisco to New York. Treasure hunters discovered her remains in 1989. Her cargo is valued at about $400 million.

THE SAN JOSE

The wreckage of this Spanish galleon has been located in the Caribbean. She set sail for Panama in 1707, loaded with gold and silver bars, doubloons (gold coins once used in Spain and Spanish America), and jewels. One month into the voyage, she was seized by pirates and sank. Most of her treasures went down with her. Her treasures are valued at more than $1 billion.

Flags

Flags are usually warning signs. Here are some of the flags you might see posted by Coast Guard stations, in yacht marinas, or flown on other boats.

FLAG	WHAT IT MEANS
Single red triangle	Weather advisory, winds up to 38 mph
Two red triangles	Weather advisory, winds up to 54 mph
Red square with black square inside	Storm warning, winds up to 73 mph
Two red squares with black squares inside	Hurricane warning, winds 74 mph and up
Blue and white (Alpha Flag)	Displayed by boats conducting dives
Red with white stripe	If floating on the water, divers are present
Blue with white rectangle inside	Often called "Papa," it means the ship is ready to sail, crew members return

Semaphore

The language of hand flags is used by sailors, lifeguards, locomotive engineers, and Boy Scouts to send messages. Each position of the two flags has a different meaning. Some flag positions spell out the individual letters of the alphabet. To spell out numbers, the person first waves the sign for numerals and follows it with the first ten letters of the alphabet. Why not make your own set of two-color flags and send messages to your friends?

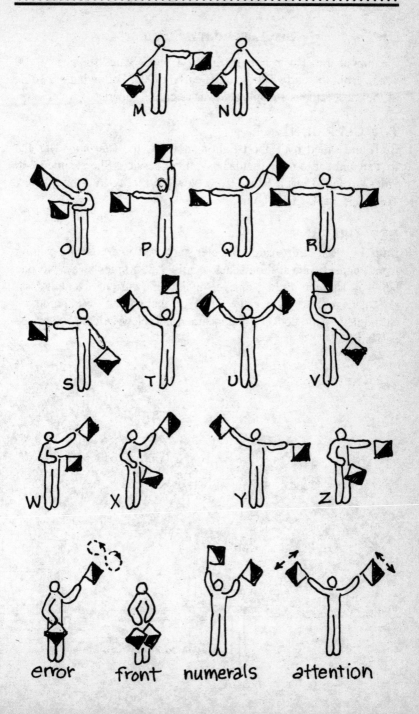

M

N

O

P

Q

R

S

T

U

V

W

X

Y

Z

error   front   numerals   attention

Six Legendary Steamers

Steamboat travel was popular in the United States for nearly 100 years, from the early 1800s to the early 1900s. Following are some of the most famous steamboats ever to cruise America's waterways.

THE CLERMONT

Built and sailed by Robert Fulton in 1807, the *Clermont* was the first steamboat to offer regular passenger service. She steamed 240 miles up the Hudson River from New York City to Albany, New York, and back in 63 hours.

NEW ORLEANS

Built in 1810, this paddlewheeler surprised everyone by sailing from Pennsylvania to Louisiana, nearly 1,800 miles away. No one believed she could chug upriver against the current. Nonetheless, she managed to "shoot the Falls of the Ohio," weathered an earthquake while docked, and steamed into New Orleans to service passengers.

THE NATCHEZ AND THE ROBERT E. LEE

The 1870 race between these two steamers is legendary. Both were known for their speed. The *Lee* won the race by steaming from New Orleans (Louisiana) to St. Louis (Missouri) in 3 days, 18 hours, and 14 minutes, at an average speed of 11.58 miles per hour. The record still stands.

THE GREAT EASTERN

This magnificent steamer was so large and heavy that tugboats couldn't move her. So she was launched when the tide rose. Built as a cruise ship in 1850, she could carry 4,000 passengers at speeds averaging 15 knots. From 1865 to 1873, she lay transoceanic telegraph cables. When she was broken up in 1889, wreckers found the skeleton of a man wedged between her double hull.

THE J. M. WHITE

Built in 1844, this luxury liner was the fastest side-wheeler on the river. On one of her first voyages she steamed from New Orleans (Louisiana) to St. Louis (Missouri) in 3 days, 23 hours, 9 minutes. The record stood until 1870, when the *Robert E. Lee* beat her time by only a few hours.

Thirteen Famous Ships You Can Visit

Balcultha (square-rigger)   San Francisco, California
Constitution (frigate)   Boston, Massachusetts
Cutty Sark (British tea clipper)   Greenwich, England
H.M.S. Victory (Nelson's flagship)   Portsmouth, England
Intrepid (Aircraft Carrier)   New York Harbor, New York
Mayflower II (replica of original Mayflower)   Plymouth, Massachusetts

Queen Mary (British luxury liner) Long Beach, California
Sprague (stern-wheeler) Vicksburg, Mississippi
Ticonderoga (side-wheeler) Shelburne, Vermont
Turbinia (first turbine vessel) Newcastle, England
U.S.S. North Carolina (World War II battleship) Wilmington, North Carolina
U.S.S. Olympia (Dewey's flagship) Philadelphia, Pennsylvania
Vasa (17th-century warship) Stockholm, Sweden

SUBMARINES

The first submarine looked nothing like the sleek Navy vessels cruising the waterways today. Designed in 1620 by Dutchman Cornelius Drebbel, it was a wooden rowboat covered with animal hides. Most modern submarines are nuclear-powered, dive 100 feet or deeper in less than a minute, and are able to remain submerged for about 60 days. What's more, they can cruise faster underwater than on the surface. The average surface speed is 20 knots; underwater cruising averages 30 knots.

Submarine Bits

- The first war submarine was built by David Bushnell in 1775. Called the *Turtle*, it was shaped like an egg, sat one person, and was powered by a hand-cranked propeller. It was used in the Revolutionary War in 1776, but failed to sink any ships.
- The first submarine to sink a ship was *Nautilus*, built by American inventor Robert Fulton in 1800. It was only 21 feet long, and was covered with copper. This submarine is said to have been the inspiration for Jules Verne's famous novel, *20,000 Leagues Under the Sea*.
- The world's largest fleet of submarines—280—is in the Soviet Union. Not all are nuclear-powered.
- The U.S. Navy's fleet currently includes 134 submarines, all nuclear-powered. Several more are being built.

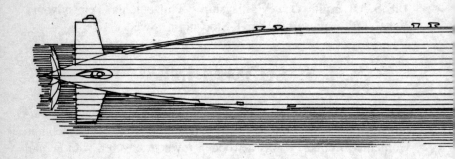

Major Types of U.S. Submarines

Fast attack submarines can destroy surface ships as well as other submarines. Ranging in length from 250 feet to 360 feet, they rely on sonar to navigate underwater. Radar and periscopes are used to spot ships on the surface. These submarines are armed with torpedoes and guided missiles. Los Angeles Class subs are the largest, fastest and most well equipped submarines in America. They carry a crew of about 110.

Ballistic missile submarines are larger than attack-type models, measuring about 560 feet overall. Each carries 24 Trident missiles, which have firing ranges of 4,000 miles. The missiles, which are fired underwater, are accurate enough to pick out a single building on a large city block. During times of peace, the submarines patrol the seas, watching submarines from other countries. Their mission is to go unnoticed.

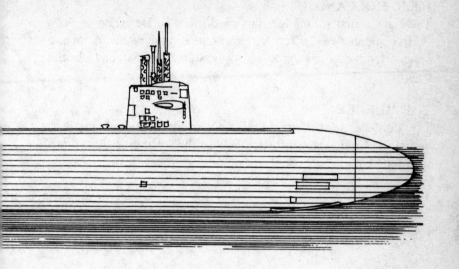

Submarines Hall of Fame

U.S.S. NAUTILUS
The *Nautilus* was the first nuclear-powered submarine, and the first sea vessel to reach the North Pole. On August 1, 1958, she dipped 750 feet below the Arctic ice at Point Barrow, Alaska, and surfaced 96 hours later after steaming 1,803 miles under the ice. Today she is a national historic landmark and can be seen at the Naval Submarine Base, New London, in Groton, Connecticut.

GERMAN U-BOATS
The most feared of all submarines during World War I and certainly the deadliest. In 1915, a German U-boat torpedoed the British ocean liner *Lusitania* and attacked many U.S. merchant ships. Cruising underwater during World War II in large groups known as *wolf packs*, U-boats sank hundreds of warships. America's war fleet destroyed many of these submarines when radar and sonar were finally developed.

U.S.S. HOLLAND
The Navy's first submarine, launched in 1900. Designed by John P. Holland, she was 53 feet long and cruised underwater at about 6 knots. Her power was provided by gasoline engines and electric batteries.

THE HUNLEY
This Confederate submarine sank the warship *Housatonic* in 1864, during the Civil War. Historians believe the submarine went down with the ship.

TRITON
The first submarine to travel around the world underwater. In 1960, she covered more than 36,000 miles in 76 days.

CHAPTER 6

All Sorts of Cycles

• •

It's a fact: at the turn of the century more people rode tricycles than bicycles! What type of cycle will be popular when the century turns again in 2000? That remains to be seen. Meanwhile, you may find a few hints in this chapter. Read on to find out all about practically every bike, trike, motorcycle, and unicycle ever invented.

BICYCLES AND TRICYCLES

Did you know that the first bicycle was actually a hobby horse, a toy horse on wheels? Created by Comte de Sirva of France in 1791, it was constructed of wood and had two wheels and a seat. Of course, since there were no pedals the rider sat on the "saddle" and "walked" it with his feet. Sirva called his invention the *walkalong*. Read on to learn more about the first bicycles and their inventors, the famous races of yesterday and today, and the riders who pedaled them to victory.

Bike Bits

- The first bicycle with pedals was built by Kirkpatric Macmillan, a Scottish blacksmith, in 1838. The rear wheel was driven by a rod connected to the pedals. Macmillan was the first person to get a traffic ticket for riding a bike, when he accidentally ran over a child.
- Full-size tricycles were popular in the late 1800s because people found them easier to balance than two-wheelers. One favorite style was built with two large wheels in front and a small single wheel in back—the opposite of modern trikes.
- Some early tricycles were so heavy that people could barely lift them. One "lightweight" model built especially for women weighed 110 pounds.
- American H. T. Butler is considered the father of the tandem (two-rider) cycle. He made sketches of his machine in the late 1860s.
- The father of the bicycle industry is James Starley, who in 1870 patented the "Ariel" (see Penny Farthing under "Memorable Bikes and Trikes"). The rider's seat was mounted above the high front wheel and people were always falling off. Even funnier, the bike came with instructions on how to fall without getting hurt!
- The first pneumatic (air-filled) tires were developed in 1881 by J. B. Dunlop. He fitted the tires to his son's tricycle.
- Bicycle-mounted soldiers, called Cycle Corps, were a common sight in the late 1800s. Soldiers equipped their bikes with lanterns and rifle holders.
- The first American-made bike was the *Columbia,* manufactured by Colonel Albert Pope.
- The first folding bicycles were introduced around 1900. They were used by paratroopers who had parachuted from airplanes.
- Riders in the early 1900s dreamed up all sorts of crazy ideas for their vehicles. A New York haircutter mounted a barber's chair onto his tricycle and became a traveling barbershop.
- The largest bicycle ever built was more than 35 feet long, weighed more than half a ton, and sat 22 riders. It was built by the Rickman brothers of England in 1968.

- *Cruisers,* one-speed bikes, are commonly called *paperboy bikes.*
- Today about 95 million Americans ride bikes; more than 2 million ride to school or work on one every day.
- Shanghai, China, is considered the bicycling center of the world, where more than 2.5 million bike trips take place daily.
- More than 75 percent of all bicycle-related accidents involve head injuries. So wear your helmet!

Memorable Bikes and Trikes

Following are some of the early designs for bicycles and tricycles.

THE BONESHAKER

Originally called the *velocipede,* this was one of the first modern-looking bicycles. Invented in France in 1866, it was constructed of wood and metal; its two wheels were almost the same size. Riders were quick to nickname it the *boneshaker* because it shook their bones when they bumped over the roads.

THE PENNY FARTHING

Britain introduced the "Ariel" in 1873. Known as a *high-wheeler,* or *Penny Farthing,* the front wheels were almost as tall as a man; the back wheels were as small as those on modern tricycles. Balancing and steering were major problems, and riders often fell off.

THE SWIFT LADIES

Also known as the *Ladies' Dandy Horse,* this bike was built especially for women. The connecting bar was placed low so the woman's fashionably long skirt could be lifted over it. It was popular in the early 1800s.

THE HOWE TRICYCLE

The rider's seat of this giant tricycle was centered between two huge wheels; the front wheel was small. It was guided with two hand levers and moved with pedal power. It was popular with adults in the late 1800s.

THE AMERICAN STAR

This bike had a small front wheel and a seat mounted over the large back wheel. Problem was, every time a rider hit a bump, he fell off the back of the bike. It was invented in 1880.

THE ROVER SAFETY

The *Rover Safety* was the first modern-looking bicycle. The wheels were driven by chains and were exactly the same size. Mass-produced in 1885, it was lightweight and easy to ride; its seat could be raised or lowered.

THE BICYCLE BUILT FOR TWO

Tandems—bicycles built for two—were more popular at the turn of the century than they are today. One model, called the *Club Convertible,* was equipped with four wheels: two small wheels on either end, and two large wheels on either side. The rider's seat was centered between the high side wheels.

THE MONOCYCLE

If you've ever rolled inside a tire, you can imagine how it felt to ride the *Monocycle*. Riders pedaled a three-wheeled contraption that was housed inside a large outer wheel. Turning and stopping was solved by the rider by leaning from side to side or back and forth.

THE SHOWER UNICYCLE

What better way to bathe than to pedal the water from the tap? This *velocipede* was mounted in a shower tray. The harder the rider pedaled, the more water came out of the spout. The unicycle was displayed at a bike show in Paris, France, but never caught on with riders.

THE ICE-VELOCIPEDE

If bikes can be pedaled on the road, why not over ice? The *ice-velocipede* had spiked runners in the rear and a large tire in front. Riders used them to pedal over frozen lakes in winter.

THE DECEMTUPLE

This American-made bike was built for ten riders. There were ten separate seats, ten sets of pedals, and two wheels—one in front and one in back. Built in 1896, it's now on exhibit in a museum in Michigan.

Bicycle Racing

The first known U.S. bicycle race was held in Boston's Beacon Park in 1878. The winner—C. A. Parker, a student—pedaled a distance of 3 miles in 12 minutes, 27 seconds. Today American

cyclists are among the top racers in the world. At the 1984 Olympic games, the U.S. cycling team took four gold medals, three silvers, and two bronzes, the first medals in cycling since 1912. In 1986, 1989, and again in 1990, Greg LeMond of Reno, Nevada, became the only American to win the famous 2,000-mile-long Tour de France championship. His time in 1989 was 87 hours, 38 minutes, 35 seconds.

Trackside Trivia

- To prove that bicycles were the fastest-wheeled vehicles, Charles M. Murphy raced his bike behind a train in New York. On June 30, 1896, he pedaled a mile in less than 58 seconds and was nicknamed "Mile-a-Minute Murphy."
- In 1899 the fastest bicycle rider in the world was Major Taylor, the first African-American athlete to compete in the World Championships, in Montreal, Canada.
- Olympic bicycles are specially built and cost as much as $45,000 each.
- Disc wheels, the zoomy-looking solid wheels on some racing bikes, are not just for show. Racers like them because the solid mass cuts down wind resistance.
- Track racing bikes do not have brakes.
- Bicycle racing became a sport in 1883, but did not become an Olympic sport until 1896.
- In 1985 John Howard sped more than 152 miles per hour over Bonneville Salt Flats on a specially built bike weighing only 46 pounds. To cut down wind resistance, he rode behind a race car that had a large tail.
- The fastest person to ride the 3,000-mile Race ACross America (RAMM) was Paul Solon in 1989. He rode 2,910 miles from California to New York in 8 days, 8 hours, 45 minutes. The female record holder is Elaine Mariolle, who rode 3,107.3 miles in 8 days, 9 hours, 47 minutes, in 1986.
- *Motocross* is a combination of the words *motorcycle* and *cross-country*. The race is run on a man-made track that includes jumps, bumps, and turns. Riders compete on specially designed, off-road motorcycles.

- BMX is short for bicycling motocross. The sport is almost exactly like motocross, only riders compete on bicycles.
- The fastest average speed pedaled in the 345-mile Bordeaux to Paris, France, race is 29 miles per hour, set by Herman van Springle of Belgium, in 1981.
- The Ore-Da Women's Challenge is America's longest cycling event for women. The race covers a distance of 661 miles and is run for 17 days over mountainous terrain in Idaho. Rebecca Twigg, an Olympic silver medalist, won the first three championships, in 1984, 1985, and 1986.

Gold Medal Winners

The following teams and individuals took gold medals in cycling at the summer Olympic Games in 1988.

EVENT	WINNER(S)	COUNTRY
Women's Sprint	Erika Saloumiae	Soviet Union
Women's Road Race	Monique Knol	Netherlands
Men's Sprint	Lutz Hesselich	East Germany
4,000 Individual Pursuit	Gintaoutas Umaras	Soviet Union
4,000 Team Pursuit	Soviet Cycling Team	Soviet Union
50 Kilometer Race	Dan Forst	Denmark
1K Time Trial	Alexandr Kiritchenko	Soviet Union
100K Team Time Trial	East German Cycling Team	East Germany
Road Race	Olaf Ludwig	East Germany

Cycle Talk

Following is a partial list of common racing words and their meanings.

Attack A sudden pulling away from one rider or a group of riders.

Bonk When a rider runs out of energy; sometimes called "hitting the wall."

Breakaway Single or group of riders who leave the main pack behind.

Circuit race Racing for several laps on a course at least 2 miles long.

Criterium Racing for several laps on a course of 2 miles or shorter. Good sprinting skills are important in this event.

Derailleur Device that moves the chain from gear to gear.

Drafting Rider who rides into a pocket of moving air behind the rider in front, allowing the second rider to pedal more easily.

Field The main group of riders, sometimes called the *bunch* or *pack*.

Flyer A surprise attack.

Force the pace When a rider moves faster to force the pack to move faster.

Hammering Riding hard.

Hook Movement of rider who moves his or her back wheel against the front wheel of the trailing bike.

Jam A long chase.

Kick Final burst of speed, usually for the sprint.

Miss-and-out A track race where the last rider to complete the lap is out. The winner is the last remaining rider.

Motor pacing Cyclists who ride one behind the other, usually following a motorcycle or motor scooter.

Prime *(pronounced PREEM)* A sprint within a race for cash prizes or points.

Pull To take a turn at the front of the group and keep the same speed.

Road bike Bike used for road racing and training.

Sew-up Tire used by racing cyclists. The tube is sewn so that the tube and tire are all one piece. Tires are made of silk, weigh 150–200 grams, and cost from $50 to $70 each.

Slipstream The area of least wind resistance behind a rider.

Sitting in Sitting closely behind the rider in front.

Squirrelly Describes a nervous or unstable rider.

Stage race Racing event that includes several one-day races over a period of time. The winner is the rider with the best overall scores.

Take a flyer To suddenly ride off the front.

Tempo riding Training at a very fast pace.

Velodrome Racing track that has sloping turns and flat straightaways.

Wind-out A sprint that develops gradually, usually with more than one lap left to go.

SOURCE: U.S. CYCLING FEDERATION.

MOTORCYCLES

As funny as it sounds, the first motorcycles had three wheels and were powered by giant steam engines. Motorcycles have been traveling roads and highways around the world for more than a century. Modern motorcycles offer quick, fun, cheap transportation. And they're very popular with racers. Read about some of the strangest bikes ever built, the hottest and fastest modern motorcycles, and all about the daredevils who race them.

Cycle Scoop

- The first motorized bike was built by automobile designer Gottlieb Daimler in 1885. His *Einspur* was built of wood and iron and powered by a ½ horsepower engine that sped 12 miles per hour. It burned in a fire in 1903.

- Aviation pioneer Glenn Curtiss earned the title "World's Fastest Human" when he sped more than 137 miles per hour at Ormond Beach, Florida, in 1907. At the time a Rolls-Royce *Silver Ghost* (a car) had a top speed of 63 miles per hour.

- Motorcycle racers are superstars in Europe. At present the most famous road racer is Eddie Lawson, an American, who has won the world championship title four times.

- *Sidecars*, wheeled seats attached to motorcycles, were introduced by W. G. Graham in 1903. They were an instant hit because passengers liked them better than riding behind the driver. Sidecars came in all shapes, sizes, and colors and were equipped with foot warmers and fold-down seats. Modern sidecars are still very popular in Japan.

- Famed stuntman Evel Knievel broke more than 400 bones during his career.

- An *enduro* is not a race. The event is run over rough terrain on courses ranging from 50 to 150 miles. Riders keep steady pace and earn points while passing checkpoints along the course. The rider earning the most points is the winner.

- *Motocross* is the most popular form of motorcycle racing in America. These events are open to any "qualified" rider between the ages of 6 and 60.

- The first TT (Tourist Trophy) race was won by Charles Collier of England on a *Matchless* motorcycle. His speed averaged 40 miles per hour. The modern speed record was set in 1984 by Joey Dunlop, who sped more than 118 miles per hour on a *Honda*.

- "Observed Trails" competitions are the most dangerous of all motorcycle races. These courses are run over slippery banks, rivers, in deep sand, muddy pits, steep hills, and ramps. Performance is more important than speed.

Three Hot Motorcycles

Here are the three fastest motorcycles in the world.

MOTORCYCLE	1/4-MILE SPEED	SECONDS	TOP END SPEED
Yamaha FZ1000	135.13 mph	10.40	163 mph
Kawasaki ZX-10 Ninja 1000	134.12 mph	10.47	163 mph
Suzuki GSX-R1100	131.77 mph	10.51	159 mph

ROAD TESTED BY *CYCLE WORLD* MAGAZINE, 1989.

Cycling Superstars

FASTEST SPEED
Donald Vesco of California rode his 21-foot-long *Lightning Bolt* over Bonneville Salt Flats, Utah, at an average speed of more than 318 miles per hour, in 1978.

LONGEST JUMP
Chris Bromham jumped 214 feet on a Yamaha in 1986. In 1923 the record jump was 62 feet, jumped by Piet Lievaart of South Africa.

MOST FAMOUS RIDER
Retired stuntman Evel Knievel, famed for soaring over long rows of trucks and cars. His attempt at jumping across Idaho's Snake River made history. The canyon is twice as wide as a football field is long (600 feet) and sports a roaring river at the bottom. Knievel's motorcycle was fitted with rocket-powered engines and a parachute in case of accident. As it turned out, the parachute opened as he shot off the ramp and he floated safely into the canyon, where he was rescued by a helicopter. The stunt earned him $6 million.

MOST DANGEROUS RACE COURSE

The 37-mile-long Mountain Circuit on the Isle of Man, off the coast of England, site of the famous Auto-Cycle Union Tourist Trophy (TT) race, held since 1907. This hilly course features a climb of 1,400 feet and 264 narrow corners and curves. The course is so dangerous that some of the world's top racers won't drive on it.

FASTEST ACROSS THE U.S.

Joseph Railton traveled 2,934 miles in just 2 days, 16 hours, in 1985. His speed averaged 45 miles per hour.

Memorable Motorcycles

Early motorcycle designers couldn't decide where to put the engine and the rider. Seats have been everywhere from high above both wheels to in front of the wheels. The engine has also moved around. At one time it was housed above the front wheel, under the seat, and in special compartments that trailed behind the bike. Following are some of the most unusual motorcycles ever built.

THE PHAETON MOTO-CYCLE

In 1884 American Lucius Copeland fitted a steam engine to his *American Star* bicycle and created the *Phaeton Moto-Cycle*. Historians say the engine weighed less than 20 pounds, which was light for a steam engine. Unfortunately, Copeland was the only person who could ride it.

THE INDIAN

This motorcycle was the most popular road and racing cycle in the early 1900s. By 1913 about 400 *Indians* were rolling off the assembly line every day. Thousands of soldiers used them as transport during World War II. Although the original company folded in 1953, two American companies still build motorcycles bearing the *Indian* brand name.

THE PETROL CYCLE

Built by English inventor Edward Butler in 1888, this motorcycle was one of the first fitted with a gasoline engine. It looked like a backward tricycle; the seat was mounted between the two front wheels, and a third wheel trailed behind. Riders guided the machine with a steering handle.

THE STEAM TRICYCLE

It was only a matter of time before someone fitted a tricycle with a steam engine and called it a motorcycle. Built in England in the late 1800s, it was actually a tricycle built for two. Riders sat side by side on a seat centered between two large wheels. The small front wheel was steered by a handle. Unfortunately, the steam engine was mounted directly below the riders' seat and often exploded, blasting the riders right off the trike.

THE HARLEY-DAVIDSON ELECTRA GLIDE

Developed by William Harley and Arthur Davidson, *Harley-Davidson* motorcycles are known for their power, speed, and size. A wide variety of touring and racing models have been built over the years. The *Electric Glide* model was used by American police in the late 1960s. It was big, comfortable, powerful, and the only motorcycle built with a reverse gear. Although it had a fast top-end speed, it was not built for racing.

UNICYCLES

Unicycles have only one wheel and no handlebars. Riders sit in a banana-shaped seat and control the cycle by leaning their weight back and forth. Backward and forward movements are controlled by pushing the pedals. Because they're fun to ride and perfect for doing tricks, unicycles have long been popular with kids, stunt riders, and circus performers.

Unicycle Trivia

- The first unicycles appeared in the late 1800s. They were ridden by circus performers who juggled balls and did all kinds of tricks.
- Unicycles taller than 6 feet are called *giraffe cycles*. They're made by hand. Shorter unicycles are made by Schwinn, Columbia, and other bike makers, and can be bought in some bike stores.
- Unicycles often appear in parades, at live shows, and at circuses. Some people even play basketball while riding them.
- Some unicycles are as tall as 18 feet, while others are shorter than 2 feet.
- Poplar unicycle tricks include long jumps, riding down steps, and riding on narrow rampways.

CHAPTER 7

Fun Vehicles Just for Kids

Kids always have great ideas about how to get from place to place. In fact, in 1988 American toy manufacturers sold $608 million worth of "ride-on" toys, including scooters, wagons, trikes, sleds, and toy cars, just to name a few. In this chapter you'll read about the fun vehicles kids ride almost every day—roller skates, skateboards, soap boxes, and others. Here you'll also find a guide to the scariest roller coasters in America and learn about some fabulous trips you can take on real covered wagons, canoes, and more.

ROLLER SKATES

Did you know that the first roller skates were in-line skates—wheels all in one row. They were invented more than 200 years ago by a Dutch ice skater who couldn't wait for winter to begin. This man simply nailed wooden spools to strips of wood and attached them to his shoes! Keep reading for more on the funny skates of yesterday and the zoomy blades of today.

Little-Known Facts About Skates

- Roller skates gained attention for the first time in 1750 when Joseph Merlin, a British instrument maker, went to a masked ball wearing metal-wheeled boots. He was playing a violin when he rolled onto the dance floor!
- The first side-by-side or conventional skate was invented by James Leonard Plimpton of Medford, Massachusetts, in 1863. In-line skates soon disappeared.
- Ball-bearing wheels first appeared on skates built in 1880.
- Some early skates had as many as eight wheels, all made of wood.
- One inventor fitted a gasoline engine to his skates and zoomed everywhere.
- The Roller Skating Rink Operators Association of the United States was formed in 1937 to promote amateur roller skating. This organization developed the rules for competitions in figure skating, free style, and dance skating.

- In 1958 the second most popular Girl Scout merit badge was in roller skating. The most popular badge was swimming.

- Indoor roller rinks were popular until the 1970s. Unfortunately, many of them were torn down or converted to ice-skating rinks.
- Puck Hockey, a game like ice hockey, is played on roller skates.
- Polyurethane wheels were first introduced in 1973 and changed the way people skated.

Let's Go Blading—On Rollerblades™

Blading is fun and the hottest skate sport in America today. Rollerblades™ ''in-line'' skates were developed by two Minnesota brothers in 1980. They sold the skates to hockey players and to snow skiers, as a tool for training in summer. Today, Rollerblades™ are not only a ''cross-training'' tool for sportspeople but a great tool for exercising, racing, trick skating, and just plain fun. Team Rollerblade™, a team of professional skaters, skates up a storm at theme parks all over the country. Watch for them in your city.

Fun Ways to Travel to School

Here are some of the ways kids travel to school. Add your own ideas to the list.

Pogo Stick	Stilts	Snow Mobile
Scooter	Walking on Hands	Skipping
Skateboard	Snow Skis	Ice Skates
Wagon	Sled	Toboggan
Snowshoes	Bicycle	Unicycle
Walking Backward	Leap-frogging	Stroller
Tricycle	Snowboard	Roller skates

SKATEBOARDS

Millions of kids ride skateboards every day. They're fun to ride and completely portable. But did you know that early skateboarders kneeled instead of stood? What's more, the boards were made of wood and fitted with metal roller-skate wheels. The fun began in the 1950s when California surfers took to the sidewalks and streets. Here's where you'll learn all about early skateboards, how to build your own board, all about skateboard champs, and the funny names they've given to their tricks.

The Scoop on Skateboards

• The first commercial skateboard was the *Roller Derby*. The wooden board was painted bright red, and rolled on a steel skate wheel. Originally sold for $5.00, one in good condition today is worth 100 times that amount.
• Skateboarding became a professional sport in the mid-1970s.
• Some early skateboards were fitted with clay roller-skating wheels. Plastic wheels did not appear until the early 1970s.
• Skate parks were all the rage in the 1970s. Although they faded from view in the 1980s, experts predict they'll be back in the 1990s.

- Unlike most modern skateboards, early skateboards came in a large variety of shapes, designs, and sizes, and were built of an even larger variety of materials, including aluminum, wood, and Fiberglas. Today the parts are standardized and thus can be interchanged.
- The most popular board graphics today include Winnie the Pooh, the Cat in the Hat, elephants, totem poles, a cat chasing a bird, and a farm scene.
- The *Ollie,* a levitation trick, is one of the first and most important tricks mastered by riders. It helps kids jump on and off curbs, skim over potholes and ditches, and cruise up and down stairs.
- California is the skateboard capital of the world.
- Some skateboarders win as much as $10,000 at national contests.

How to Build a "Pro" Skateboard

Although skateboards can be purchased already assembled, most skateboarders like to buy the parts separately and build their own boards. About 95 percent of the boards themselves are "pro models," boards ridden by the champs. These boards are made of seven-ply hard rock Canadian maple, range in length from 29 to 32 inches, and are between 9 and 11 inches wide. The colorful graphics are already on the boards. Following is a list of the major parts you'll need to buy in order to assemble your own skateboard. Parts are available in sporting stores.

| Axles (trucks) | Board | Wheel Bearings |
| Wheels | Grip Tape | Bolts |

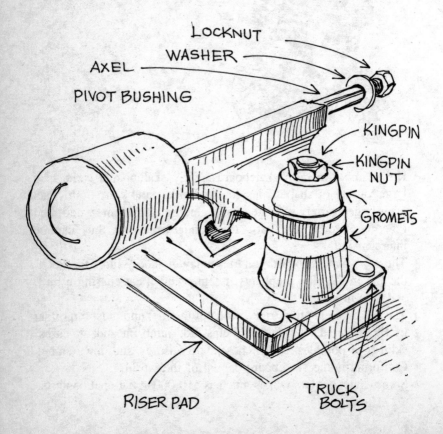

LOCKNUT
WASHER
AXEL
PIVOT BUSHING
KINGPIN
KINGPIN NUT
GROMETS
RISER PAD
TRUCK BOLTS

Must-Have Safety Equipment

The following equipment is worn by professional skateboarders to prevent injuries:

Sturdy, hightop sneakers or
   specially designed shoes
Knee pads

Elbow pads
Helmet
Wrist braces

Skateboard Champs

Here, according to the National Skateboard Association, are the hottest boarders in America.

NAME	CONTEST CATEGORY
Tony Hawk	Ramp riding
Mike Miguel	Ramp riding
Christian Hosoi	Ramp and street style
Steve Caballero	Ramp, street style, and all-around rider
Danny Way	Ramp and street style
Tony Magnusson	Ramp riding: performed the world's highest "air"—11 feet—in 1989.
Rodney Mullen	Ramp riding

Skateboard Tricks with Funny Names

There are as many skateboard tricks as there are riders. Following is a partial list of some of the most popular tricks.

Stink Bug
Toothpick
Feeble
Christ Air

Indy Nose Pick
McTwist
Stale Fish
Roast Beef

Slappy
Madonna
Chinese Ollie
Japan Air

THE ALL-AMERICAN SOAP BOX DERBY

The first soap box racers were built of peach crates and had bread boxes for hoods. Kids dragged them up hilltops and coasted down as fast as they could. Today boys and girls build fancy cars and compete at official derby tracks in cities all over America. Local winners race at the World Championship All-American Soap Box Derby held annually at *Derby Downs* in Akron, Ohio. Following are some fascinating facts about the first races, tips on how to enter a local race and build your own car, and where to write for more information.

Soap Box Trivia

- The sport was born in 1933 in Dayton, Ohio, when news photographer Myron Scott chanced upon a group of boys racing their home-built cars.
- The World Championship All-American Soap Box Derby has been run every August since 1934. Although the first national race was held at Dayton, it was moved to Akron in 1935 because of its central location and hilly terrain.
- *Derby Downs* is a specially built 954-foot track site. Cars must be started by gravity from a standstill, on either the track or a starting ramp. Pushing is not allowed. Racers are allowed one trial run before the race.
- The first winner of the All-American was Bob Turner, age 11, of Indiana.
- The first girl to take the World Championship title was Karen Stead, age 11, of Morrisville, Pennsylvania, who won in 1975.
- Some soap box cars cruise as fast as 35 miles per hour.
- According to the rules, racers must first enter and win a local race before competing at the All-American in Akron.
- The goal of the Soap Box Derby program is to "teach youngsters some of the basic skills of workmanship, the spirit of competition and the perseverance to continue a project once it has begun."
- Racers competing at the All-American are ushered into town by a police escort and introduced to the crowds at a welcoming ceremony.
- Championship racers bunk together at Derbytown, a YMCA camp near Akron. During the week of festivities, racers take part in parades and many other special activities.
- Both national and local races are run on a system of elimination by heats. The winner is the car whose nose crosses first over the finish line.
- Many celebrities attend the All-American and take part in the festivities. Famous people who have attended in past years include Tom Hanks (from the movie *Big*), Kevin Wixted (from TV's "Growing Pains"), Punky Brewster, Bobby Allison (race car champion), George Takei ("Star Trek"), and Chad Allen ("My Two Dads").

- Race day activities are kicked off with a special racers' parade followed by the *Oil Can Trophy Race,* in which stars race in large Derby cars.

The Prizes

There are prizes galore for every racer at the All-American. The top three winners in the Kit Car Division receive trophies and prizes. The top three winners in the Masters Division receive scholarships of $5,000 (first place), $3,000 (second place), and $2,000 (third place), plus trophies. All contestants receive the following:

Official Derby watch   Official Derby racing jacket
Official Derby T-shirt   Official Derby hat

How to Enter a Local "Kit Car Division" Race

There are two major divisions in both the local and the All-American competitions: the Kit Car and the Master divisions. Some of the rules and requirements for the Kit Car Division are listed below. Rules for the Master Division, for kids 12 through 16, are available from the All-American.

GENERAL REQUIREMENTS
Write to: The All-American Soap Box Derby, Derby Downs, P.O. Box 7233, Akron, Ohio 44306, and ask for the official "Soap Box Derby Activities Book" and the "Soap Box Derby Rule Book." Everything you need to know is listed in these books. A registration form is also included.
Age: Boys and girls 9 through 16. Kids between the ages of 9 and 11 are required to compete in the Kit Car Division. Eleven-year-olds who have already won a Kit Car race or have competed at the All-American may race in the Masters Division.
Eligibility: You may enter one car per year in only one division. You must participate in the official Soap Box Derby *closest* to your permanent residence.

Cars must be purchased from the International Soap Box Derby, Inc., and built according to the plan sheets. The car's body may be constructed of wood, or you may purchase the Junior Jetstar™ Fiberglas Body Shell. Wheels are separate.

Length: No longer than 80 inches, or 80¹⁄₁₆ inches with official Z-glass™ wheels.

Height: No less than 14 inches high.

Width: No less than 13 inches and no more than 28 inches.

Weight: Combined weight of the car and driver cannot exceed 220 pounds with steel wheels; 206 pounds with Z-glass™ wheels.

GENERAL RULES

- You must drive the car you build.
- Your parents or another adult may help you with cutting the floorboards, drilling the axles, and aligning the car. An adult may also show you how to lay out and cut various parts, but you must complete the construction by yourself.
- You are required to wear a shirt, trousers, rigid sole shoes, and an official racing helmet during all competitions.
- Windshields are not permitted, nor is glass of any type.

RIDING JUST FOR FUN

OK, so Ferris wheels and roller coasters don't take you anywhere except up and down. But who's complaining? There are about 600 theme parks in America and all of them are stuffed with rides. Here are some fascinating facts about two of the most popular rides—Ferris wheels and roller coasters—plus your personal guide to the scariest coasters in the U.S.

Original Ferris Wheel. World's Columbian Exposition 1893

Ferris Wheels

Ferris wheels have been thrilling kids for nearly a century. Modern wheels average 40 to 50 feet high, carry 12 to 16 cars, and can operate in winds up to 60 miles per hour. Following are three of the most famous Ferris wheels ever built.

THE ORIGINAL

The first Ferris wheel was built in 1893 by George W. Ferris of Illinois. Ferris, for whom the wheel is named, built it for the World's Columbian Exposition held in Chicago. The wheel was 250 feet in diameter and carried 36 cars. Unlike modern cars which seat 2 riders, these cars held 60 people—a total load of 2,160 riders! Weighing 150 tons, the giant wheel was dismantled and sold for scrap in 1904.

LARGEST EVER BUILT

The wheel on this enormous machine was 300 feet in diameter. It was built in 1897 and put on display in London, England. Ten of its 40 gondolas could be ridden only by rich people.

LARGEST MODERN FERRIS WHEEL

Japan's *Giant Peter,* standing 278 feet high. With its 46 cars, it can seat more than 350 riders.

Roller Coasters

Everybody loves roller coasters. In fact, did you know that about 3,000 people are members of the American Coaster Enthusiasts, a club for roller coaster riders? The first American roller coaster was called the Switchback Pleasure Gravity Railroad. It was built at Coney Island, New York, in 1884. Today there are more than 200 coasters in the U.S. Following is a partial list of the most famous coasters in the world and where you can ride them.

World Famous Scream Machines

LONGEST RIDE
The "Beast," at Kings Island in Cincinnati, Ohio. The ride offers 3 minutes and 40 seconds of thrills and chills on a track that's 1.4 miles (7,400 feet) long. Eight hundred feet of the track rip through dark tunnels. The coaster is spread over 34 acres of land.

MOST G-FORCE
The "Loch Ness Monster" at Busch Gardens in Williamsburg, Virginia, with a G-force seven times that of the Earth's gravity. Riders say they feel like they're being launched into space.

FASTEST AND LONGEST FIRST DROP
The "Magnum XL 200" at Cedar Point in Sandusky, Ohio, with a vertical drop of 205 feet, the longest in coaster history. It's also the world's fastest, screaming around corners at 72 miles per hour.

TALLEST VERTICAL LOOP
"Viper" at Magic Mountain in California, with 3 loops, including the world's tallest, at 140 feet. This coaster features batwing turns that cars take at an awesome 70 miles per hour.

TALLEST
The "Moonsault Scramble," at Fujikyu Highland Park in Japan, rising 246 feet high at its tallest point. It reaches speeds faster than 65 miles per hour.

MOST TWISTS
The "Pipeline," now under construction in Utah. This coaster will run on flexible tracks, which allow the cars to twist, rock, spin, and turn upside-down. It is due to open in the 1990s.

MOST FAMOUS
The "Cyclone," a wooden coaster opened at Coney Island, New York, in 1927, and remodeled in 1967. It also offers the most expensive ride, at $3.00 per ticket.

TALLEST AND FASTEST WOODEN COASTER
"Colossus," at Six Flags Magic Mountain in Valencia, California. Standing 114 feet tall, cars rip over the tracks at 55 miles per hour.

Awesome American Coasters

Here's a partial list of some of the scariest roller coasters in the U.S.

ARIZONA
"Big Surf," located in Tempe, boasts the world's largest man-made surf-style pool.

CALIFORNIA
"Space Mountain," an indoor coaster, and the legendary "Matterhorn," are just two of the thrills you'll enjoy at **Disneyland** in Anaheim.

Take your pick at **Six Flags Magic Mountain** in Valencia. You can choose from the double-track "Colossus," the stand-up "Shock Wave," the suspended "Ninja," "Revolution," which is built into the mountain, and "Viper," sporting the tallest vertical loop.

"Boomerang" with three loops, the "Roaring 20's Corkscrew," and "Montezooma's Revenge" are three rides offered at Buena Park's **Knott's Berry Farm.**

COLORADO
"Twister," famed for its spooky tunnel, is a special treat at Denver's **Elitch Gardens Amusement Park.**

FLORIDA
Enjoy a chilling ride and special effects aboard the enclosed "Space Mountain" coaster at **Walt Disney World** in Lake Buena Vista.

ILLINOIS
Six Flags Great America, in Gurnee, boasts five heart-stoppers: "Shock Wave," "Tidal Wave," "The Demon," "The Whizzer," and "The American Eagle." The twin-track "American Eagle" claims a speed of 66.31 miles per hour with a vertical drop of 147.4 feet.

MASSACHUSETTS
The "Cyclone" at **Riverside Park** in Agawam. The first drop is 112 feet and the lift hill is 28 degrees up.

MICHIGAN
For a scary ride in the dark, hop on "Nightmare," at **Boblo Island Amusement Park** in Detroit, where you can also ride "Screamer" and "Sky Streak."

MINNESOTA
"High Roller," "Corkscrew," or "Wild Rails" are only three of the thrills you'll find at **Valleyfair Entertainment Center** in Shakopee.

MISSOURI
Dare to ride "Screaming Eagle," "Mine Train," and the new log-flume ride at **Six Flags Over Mid-America** in Eureka.

NEW YORK
Coney Island's "Cyclone," built in 1927, is a must for coaster fans worldwide.

"Comet," sitting just 20 feet from Lake Erie at Niagara Falls on **Crystal Beach,** is for thrill seekers with strong stomachs.

OHIO
Check out **Cedar Point,** home to more roller coasters than any other American theme park: nine. Here's where you'll find the "Magnum XL-200," among others.

TENNESSEE
Opryland, in Nashville, boasts a new $7 million coaster plus the "Wabash Cannonball," the "Rock 'n' Roller," and the wheeled bobsled ride "Screamin' Delta Demon."

TEXAS
Double-loop fans will love "Shock Wave," plus "Judge Roy Scream," and the "Splashwater Falls" boat ride at **Six Flags over Texas** in Arlington.

"Texas Cyclone," "Excalibur," XLR-8 (steel-suspended), and "Greezed Lightnin'," are some of the thrills you'll enjoy at Houston's **Astroworld/Waterworld.**

Wonderland Park, in Amarillo, features the "Texas Tornado," a double-loop coaster, plus "Rattlesnake River Rapids," "Riptide," and "Big Splash" water rides.

UTAH
"Fire Dragon" at **Lagoon Amusement Park** in Farmington is a double-loop coaster you won't soon forget.

WASHINGTON
For a thrilling gondola ride, board the "Dragon" at **Riverfront Park** in Spokane.

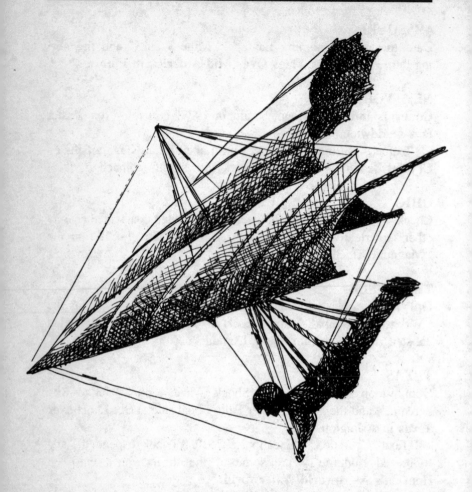

Sporty Vehicles

Over the years inventors have dreamed up ways for people to ride just for fun over land and water, and in the air. Following are some of the most popular and familiar sporty vehicles ever invented. How many have you ridden?

GLIDING WITH THE CLOUDS

Kite Flyer   Hang Glider   Ski Lift   Jetpack
Parachute   Sailplane   Gondola Car

BLASTING OVER THE WAVES

Canoes	Sailboards	Water Skis
Knee Boards	Jet Skis	Surfboards
Rafts	Skimmers	Inner Tubes
Rowboats	Water Shoes	

WHIPPING OVER ICE AND SNOW

Ice Skates	Iceboats	Downhill Skis
Cross Country Skis	Sleds	Toboggan
Ski-Bob	Snowboard	Dogsleds

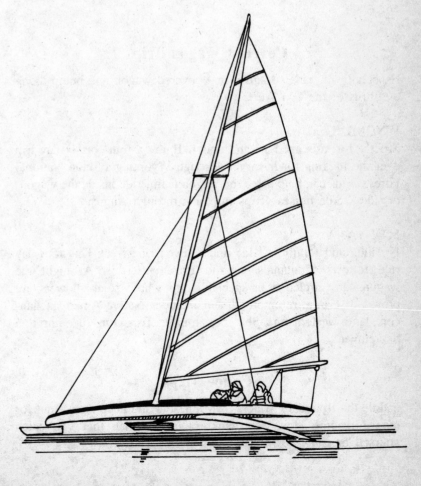

FUN TRIPS YOU CAN TAKE

Here's your chance to take a covered wagon trip, go backpacking with a llama, shoot the rapids on a raft, paddle your own canoe, or travel on horseback through the wilderness. Since 1972, thousands of kids and their families have signed up for the fabulous trips offered by the American Wilderness Experience. Following is a partial list of some of the fun adventures you can take. For more information, write to: the American Wilderness Experience, Inc., P.O. Box 1486, Boulder, Colorado, 80306, or phone: 1-800-444-0099.

Covered Wagon Trips

Especially for kids! Board a real covered wagon and bump along the trails of the Old West.

WYOMING
Strictly for kids aged 16 and under. Enjoy a four- or six-day trip over the logging roads carved through Wyoming's Teton National Forest. Kids can help drive the wagon team, ride inside the wagon, or ride saddle horses. Trips run June through August.

MONTANA
For kids and families. Kids under seven ride free! This four-day ride follows Montana's historic Bozeman Trail. At night the wagons are circled at a special camp where solar showers are provided. Campfire entertainment includes Native American dancers, and western and bluegrass music. Trips run June through September.

Canoe Trips

Paddle the Boundary Waters of Minnesota and keep an eye out for moose feeding along the banks. Dine on fish that you catch yourself or chow down at the tented campsites.

FAMILY FUN TRIP: MINNESOTA

For kids five and up and their families. Seven days and six nights of paddling, swimming, fishing, and camping along the shoreline in the Minnesota-Ontario boundary waters. The campsites are the same ones used by the French Canadian voyagers with their birchbark canoes laden with beaver pelts, and by the Ojibway Indians before them. Huddle close for the ghost stories. Trips run July through August.

Llama Trekking

Llamas are furry, friendly, and make great companions. Hike along the Continental Divide and pack your food, duffel, and camp equipment on your own personal llama.

MOUNT ZIRKEL WILDERNESS, COLORADO

For kids eight and up and their families. A five-day trek through the Colorado wilderness. Tie up your llama at night and enjoy food prepared by chefs. Campsite tents include solar showers, cots, sleeping bags, and toilets. Fish for your dinner on a raft. Trips run July through September.

SAN JUAN MOUNTAINS, COLORADO

For kids eight and up and their families. A five-day trek through the wilderness of the southwestern Rockies. Hike the sacred mountain home of the Ute Indians, along cool canyons, and through dense forests. Bed down near the glacial lakes and sleep under the stars. Trips run July through September.

Horseback Trips

Horses have served as companions and transportation for millions of years. So hop in the saddle and ride the wilderness trails of the Old West. Horses, saddles, tack, and riding instructions are included.

NEW MEXICO

A six-day adventure through the Gila Wilderness with over 3 million acres of mountain vistas, canyons, hot springs, and forests. Trips leave from El Paso, Texas, April through September.

BRIDGER-TETON BACKCOUNTRY, WYOMING

For kids eight and up and their families. Five days through the Gros Ventre Wilderness in the Wyoming Rockies. The base camp features a heated mess tent, carpeted sleeping tents, and hot showers. Spend your days on horseback exploring the surrounding territories, including Pack Saddle Pass and Turquoise Lake. Sing songs and tell ghost stories at the nightly campfires. Trips run June through September.

SUPERSTITION WILDERNESS, ARIZONA

For kids eight and up and their families. A week-long pack trip through the legendary Superstition Mountains of Arizona. The rugged desert trails are filled with cactus and deep rock canyons. At night, listen to the stories of the Lost Dutchman's gold, Spanish explorers, and renegade Apaches. Trips run February through April.

Whitewater Rafting

Here's your chance to journey through the remote world of dancing water and winding canyons on a rollicking raft. Rafts, paddles, life jackets, safety instructions, and guides are included.

DESOLATION AND GRAY CANYONS, UTAH

For kids 7 to 17. Four- and six-day journeys take rafters 84 miles down Utah's Green River and over 60 major rapids. Hike the shorelines and explore Indian sites, historic homesteads, and outlaw hideaways. Bed down at night along the white sandy beaches. Trips run May through August.

HELL'S CANYON, SNAKE RIVER, IDAHO AND OREGON
For kids 7 to 17. Three- and five-day trips on roller coaster rapids on the bottomless Hell's Canyon gorge. Enter at the Snake River, warm and clear and perfect for swimming. Camp on the sandy beaches at night. Trips run May through September.

CHAPTER 8

More Favorite People Movers

If you like riding with friends, then this chapter is for you. Here you'll read about different types of public transportation, including buses, cable cars, elevators, and more. Along the way, see if you can spot the signs that guide travelers, and keep your eyes peeled for the world's crookedest, shortest, and steepest streets and highways.

BUSES

Buses Galore

It's a fact: More than 22½ million kids ride the bus to and from school every day! But school buses aren't the only type of bus.

Some travel from town to town and state to state. Others are strictly for riding in the city. Still others can be hired or chartered for special trips or tours. Read on to find out more about buses.

Bus Bits

- The first city bus service began in Paris in 1662. Called a *Carrosses à Cinq Sous,* it sat eight people, ran on a timetable, and cost exactly five *sous* (pennies) to ride, no matter how far the rider was traveling.
- The first U.S. "buses" rolled in New York City in 1820. Drawn by horses, they carried 12 passengers, and were called *Omnibuses,* from the Latin meaning "for all."
- Buses that were comfortable did not appear until about 1920. Before this time the ride was bumpy, dust seeped through the windows and doors, and there was no heat or air-conditioning.
- *Streetcars, trolleys* and *trams* are buses that run on rails laid in the street. The early ones were called *horsecars* because they were drawn by horses. Modern trolleys are driven by electric power that comes from an overhead wire.
- Many early motor buses were nothing more than cars that had been stretched to seat more riders.
- Double-decker or two-story buses have been popular in England since the late 1800s.
- Buses are cheaper to run than airplanes, cars, or trains because they burn less fuel while traveling the same distance.
- In some states, bus service is the only type of public transportation in and out of the city.
- City buses carry more than 4½ billion passengers yearly, and travel about 1¾ billion miles.

- In the U.S. more people ride the bus than any other form of public transportation.
- Some buses seat as few as 7 passengers while others seat as many as 70.

The Scoop on School Buses

- School buses are painted bright yellow-orange to make them stand out on the road.
- In most states it's against the law for a car to pass a school bus that has stopped to let kids on or off.
- There are more than 330,000 school buses in the United States. Most are owned and operated by the schools.
- School buses became important when kids started going to schools that served several towns. Before this time, most kids walked to a nearby one-room schoolhouse.
- Anyone who wants to drive a school bus must first pass a special driving test.

Stagecoaches and Other "Buses" of the Past

Until the late 1600s, most people were still walking, hitching rides on animals, or riding in crude carts to get around. Only kings, queens, and other rich folks could afford to hire taxis or private carriages. Following are some of the vehicles people rode while traveling from place to place.

Berline   These fifteenth-century coaches looked like Cinderella's carriage. The front wheels were small, the back ones were large, and there was a separate box for the driver. It was named in honor of Berlin, which is now the capital of Germany.

Brougham   This four-wheeled carriage was the most popular form of transport during the Victorian era. It was driven by a top-hatted driver, drawn by a single horse, and was completely enclosed.

Cabriolet

The ancestor of the modern taxicab; the name was eventually shortened to *cab*. In the early 1800s, horse-drawn *cabriolets* were common on the streets of America, France, and England—and just as hard to find when people needed them as they are today.

Cisium

Also called *mail carts*, these two-wheeled carts traveled more than 50 miles a day carrying mail to the ancient Romans. Drivers often picked up hitchhikers and weary travelers.

Conestoga Wagon

These covered wagons are often confused with the *Prairie Schooners* that carried settlers across America. *Conestoga Wagons* were first built in Pennsylvania in the early 1700s and hauled heavy goods in the East. Pulled by teams of six sturdy horses, their tops were covered with canvas that had been stretched over large hoops. To keep the team moving, the driver rode the horse nearest the wagon.

phaeton

Fiacre   A horse-drawn (three horses) taxicab popular in France around the mid-1600s. The *fiacre* sat six passengers and was lighted at night by a lantern that was suspended over the driver's seat. Very fashionable.

Omnibus   The ancestor of the modern bus, the *omnibus* originated in France in the early 1800s. The early horse-drawn models seated about 20 passengers and provided cheap inner-city transport. Like many modern inner-city buses, they were always crowded and traveled through traffic jams at about 5 miles per hour.

Phaeton   This nineteenth-century open carriage was built to show off its passengers: beautifully gowned ladies and well-dressed English gentlemen. The horse's groom sat in a tiny seat at the rear. The leather top could be pulled up in times of bad weather.

Prairie Schooner   These covered wagons hauled thousands of American settlers across the rutted roads of America in the mid- to late 1800s. Like the *Conestoga Wagon,* the top was constructed of canvas and stretched over large hoops. The vehicles were uncomfortable and unstable. Wheels often bent or fell off over rough terrain.

Stagecoach   If you're a fan of westerns, you know all about stagecoaches. These large wooden vehicles were hitched to a team of horses and driven by one or two men stationed on top of the coach. Passengers sat inside on hard or thinly padded seats and prayed they would reach the next town in one piece. Like modern buses, they ran on regular schedules and carried passengers as well as mail and other goods.

Western Concord   A type of stagecoach that carried up to nine passengers inside and three on the roof, including guards. These vehicles usually followed the covered wagons across America and were drawn by a team of six or more horses. For a time they were the favorite transport of gold miners, and thus were ambushed by outlaws.

TRANSPORTATION SIGNS

Pictographs are pictures that stand for words and thoughts. And that's the whole idea—people everywhere understand their meaning without reading any words. The following signs are commonly found along highways, in picnic areas, at lake and beach resorts, and in hotels, bus depots, railroad stations, airports, campgrounds, and other public places.

gift shop

hotel information

restaurant

mail

first aid

baggage lockers

men's toilets

women's toilets

nursery

information

taxi stand

bus transportation

air transportation

car rental

rail transportation

coffee shop

bar

no smoking

no parking

parking

baggage check-in

baggage claim

customs

lost and found

currency exchange

falling rocks

drinking water

mechanic

handicapped

gas station

viewing area

campfires

picnic area

launching ramp

horse trail

bicycle trail

hiking trail

playground

no entry

elevator

CABLE CARS

Few vehicles are as fun to ride as cable cars. These colorful, clanging trolleys barrel up and down San Francisco's steep hills like roller coasters. What's more, they don't even have motors! The cars are pulled by underground cables powered by electricity and guided by drivers called *gripmen*. Andrew Hallidie, the Englishman who created the idea, called his invention the "endless ropeway." And with good reason. The cable runs on an endless loop under the street. Read on to find out more about how these amazing vehicles work.

A Roadbed of Wacky Facts

- The "roadbed" for the cable is housed in a tunnel under the street and is carried by a system of pulleys. The pulleys travel to a "Cable Barn," the powerhouse, are wound around a giant wheel, and then return to the roadbed.
- Gripmen control the car's movement with a *grip lever,* a sturdy device that grips and releases the cable. When the lever is pushed forward, the car rolls forward; when the grip is pulled back, the cable is held in place and the car stops. It takes a lot of strength to push and pull the lever.
- People everywhere were excited about Hallidie's invention, and cable car lines were built in many large cities. From 1881 until the turn of the century, millions of people rode them every day. Today, San Francisco operates the world's only cable cars, a fleet of 37 beautifully decorated vehicles.
- Although riders feel like they're speeding, the steel cable runs steadily at 9 miles per hour (792 feet per minute), so that even cars rolling downhill never go faster.
- The steel cables weigh between 15,000 and 16,800 pounds each and must be replaced every 110 to 230 days.
- Each cable car has four independent brakes: a track brake, a wheel brake, a cable brake, and a slot brake. Since the track brake is a block of soft wood and quickly wears out, it must be replaced every two to four days.

- The oldest cars now in operation are the single-ended Powell Street lines, built between 1887 and 1891.
- Many of the original cars were destroyed in a 1906 earthquake; most were rebuilt between 1906 and 1914 and still operate today.
- Gripmen wipe the front windows of the car with tobacco wrapped in a cloth pouch. The mixture leaves a thin film of oil on the window, which casts off water during rain.

ELEVATORS

Elevators are fun to ride. Here are some little-known facts about their speed and origin.

Little Known Facts About Elevators

- The average elevator travels 10,000 miles each year, rising about 800 feet in 30 seconds, or a speed of 18 miles per hour.
- The fastest passenger elevators rise 2,000 feet per minute, or nearly 23 miles per hour. Two of these speedsters can be ridden in the 60-story-high "Sunshine 60" building in Tokyo, Japan.
- In Great Britain, elevators are called *lifts*.
- Modern elevators are hoisted by cables running over pulleys at the top of the shaft. Historians believe the system was first developed by the ancient Egyptians while building the pyramids.

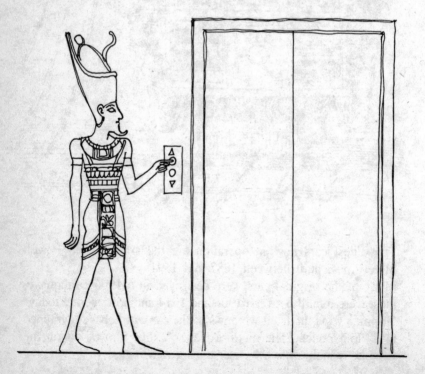

• The modern safety elevator was invented by Elisha Otis, an American engineer, in 1854.

REMARKABLE ROADS AND HIGHWAYS AROUND THE WORLD

Did you know that there are about 675,000 miles of streets in the U.S.? Of course, that wasn't always so. There weren't many paved roads around in colonial days. In fact, many roads were dirt paths. Roads paved with cobblestone and brick first appeared in the mid-1800s. By the late 1800s, many roads were paved with brick and blacktop. Today, of course, most roads are paved with concrete, blacktop, or brick. Following are some of the most remarkable roads and highways ever built.

WIDEST BOULEVARD
The Monumental Axis in Brazil. The six-lane boulevard is more than 820 feet wide.

SHORTEST STREET
McKinley Street in Bellefontaine, Ohio. Made of brick, it is only 30 feet long.

CROOKEDEST STREET
Lombard Street in San Francisco. This curvy street runs only one way—down—and sports eight 90-degree turns.

STEEPEST STREET
Canton Avenue in Pittsburgh, with a grade of 37 degrees.

LONGEST AND OLDEST TRANSCONTINENTAL HIGHWAY
The Lincoln Highway, now known as U.S. 80 and sometimes called the "Main Street of the United States." The highway stretches 3,385 miles from New York City to San Francisco, California. Concrete markers, still visible along some sections, were erected by Boy Scouts coast to coast on September 1, 1928, to celebrate its completion.

WORLD'S LONGEST ROAD TUNNEL

The St. Gotthard Road Tunnel, in Switzerland, running a total distance of 10 miles. The tunnel took 11 years to build.

MOST FAMOUS U.S. ROAD

The Cumberland Road, stretching from Cumberland, Maryland, through the 2,000- to 3,000-foot Cumberland Mountains, a natural pass through the Appalachians of Virginia, Kentucky, and Tennessee. The Cumberland Gap was the gateway west for settlers for more than a century, from 1775 to 1880. It was here that Daniel Boone blazed his "Wilderness Road" in 1775.

CHAPTER 9

Marvelous Museums

Following is a partial list of some of the most extraordinary transportation museums in America.

Aircraft

NATIONAL AIR AND SPACE MUSEUM
Independence Avenue (4th—7th street) SW
Washington, D.C.   20560
This famous museum features hundreds of planes, including the Wright brothers' *Flyer,* Charles Lindbergh's *Spirit of St. Louis,* the *Apollo 11* spacecraft, and dozens of old time warbirds.

CONFEDERATE AIR FORCE FLYING MUSEUM
Valley International Airport
Harlingen, Texas   78551
Harlingen is home to the Confederate Air Force (see Chapter 2).

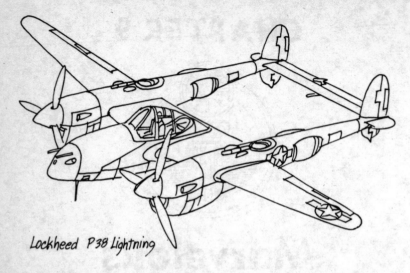

Lockheed P38 Lightning

Here you'll find a collection of more than 100 of the most famous American World War II (1939–1945) combat aircraft. The restored planes, many of which can still fly, are shown on rampways and in hangars. Don't miss the Japanese *Zero,* the German *Messerschmitt,* or the shark-mouthed *Warhawks.*

U.S. ARMY AVIATION MUSEUM
Building 6007
Fort Rucker, Alabama   36362-5000
Here you'll find the world's largest collection of helicopters. The collection includes dozens of experimental models, the *VCH-34* used by President Eisenhower, and General MacArthur's *C-121 Bataan.*

NATIONAL SOARING MUSEUM
Harris Hill, RD #3
Elmira, New York   14903
Harris Hill in Elmira is the Soaring Capital of America. The museum is near the glider field, and features a glider cockpit where visitors can listen to pilots talking as they soar overhead. Wander around and look at the artifacts and photographs and learn all about soaring.

U.S. AIR FORCE MUSEUM
Springfield St., Wright-Patterson AFB
Dayton, Ohio   45433-6518
This museum features the largest military aviation collection in the world. There are 200 antique airplanes dating back to the early 1900s and thousands of items related to aviation history.

NAVAL AIR TEST AND EVALUATION MUSEUM
Route 235 and Shangri-La Drive
Lexington Park, Maryland   20670
This museum is dedicated to the testing of naval aircraft and is the only museum of its kind in America. There are hands-on displays for kids and audiovisual presentations that trace the history of naval aircraft and tell stories of how they were tested.

Automobiles

HENRY FORD MUSEUM
20900 Oakwood Boulevard
Dearborn, Michigan   41821
More than 200 cars are featured in this enormous collection. It's here where you'll find Henry Ford's first car, the fabulous Rolls-Royce *Silver Ghost,* and the 1914 Detroit *Electric.*

HARRAH'S AUTOMOBILE COLLECTION
Glendale Road
Reno, Nevada   89504
This famous museum has the largest number of restored automobiles in the world. The collection includes a total of 1,500 antique cars, and half of them are on display. Kids can visit the restoration shops to watch workers paint and rebuild the classics.

CHEVYLAND U.S.A.
Exit 257
Elm Creek, Nebraska   68348
This museum is dedicated to Chevrolets. Practically every Chevy ever built can be found here. Most of the restored vehicles are in top running condition.

JOE WEATHERLY STOCK CAR MUSEUM
Darlington, South Carolina 29532

If you like stock cars, this museum is for you. On the site of the Darlington 500 Raceway, it's filled with the world's largest collection of stock cars. Kids can sit in the simulator and "drive" two laps in Richard Petty's Dodge Charger. Don't miss the fabulous trophy collection.

SWIGART MUSEUM
Route 22
Huntington, Pennsylvania 16653

The world's largest collection of automobile name plates and license plates can be found in this museum. Also on exhibit are 40 classic cars and a large collection of vintage headlights, horns, and car parts.

INDIANAPOLIS MOTOR SPEEDWAY HALL OF FAME MUSEUM
4790 16th Street
Speedway, Indiana 46224

The east wing of this enormous museum is filled with race cars. Eighteen of the cars are famous Indy 500 winners. Don't forget to visit the west wing, which features classic passenger cars.

Cable Cars

THE CABLE CAR MUSEUM
1201 Mason Street
San Francisco, California 94108

Fifty-seven models of vintage and modern cable cars, including the first car—built in 1873—are displayed in this museum. At the "Cable Barn," kids can watch the steel cables as they're pulled over the giant "winder" to power cars on the street. Then step outside and ride a car.

Circus Wagons

CIRCUS WORLD MUSEUM
426 Water Street
Baraboo, Wisconsin   53913
All kids love this museum. Not only does it house the world's largest collection of circus wagons, but it features daily circus shows and parades. Here you'll also find a collection of magnificent circus parade wagons. Many of them once led the parades for such famous circuses as the Ringling Brothers & Barnum and Bailey Circus.

General

NATIONAL MUSEUM OF TRANSPORT
3015 Barrett Station Road
St. Louis, Missouri   63112
This museum contains the largest collection of trolleys, streetcars, and vintage trains in America. Don't miss the antique steam locomotives, early Pullman sleeping cars, and cabooses. A must-see for train lovers.

MUSEUM OF SCIENCE AND INDUSTRY
57th Street and Lake Shore Drive
Chicago, Illinois   60637
Kids are encouraged to participate in many of the over 2,000 exhibits on display. Here you'll find a Santa Fe model railroad, a U-505 submarine, and the fantastic "Wheels of Change" exhibit.

Locomotives

NATIONAL RAILROAD MUSEUM
2285 South Broadway
Green Bay, Wisconsin   54304
If you love trains, then this museum is for you. On exhibit are more than 50 trains, including 20 steam and diesel-electric loco-

motives dating back to 1890. Photos, old railroad maps, and artifacts will help you trace the history of the great Iron Horse.

TOY TRAIN MUSEUM
Paradise Lane
Strasburg, Pennsylvania   17579
Wow! There are hundreds of toy locomotives and railroad cars in this museum. What's more, many of the trains were manufactured nearly 100 years ago. The trains run on three enormous track layouts. Don't miss the free movies.

STEAMTOWN TRAINS
Bellows Falls, Vermont   05101
There are more than 100 exhibits in this museum, including a 90-foot revolving turntable where most of the steam locomotives are displayed. Other exhibits include elegant passenger cars and cabooses. Don't forget to ride the restored steam-powered locomotive.

CENTER FOR TRANSPORTATION & COMMERCE RAILROAD MUSEUM
123 Rosenberg Street
Galveston, Texas   77554
This museum offers the largest collection of restored railroad equipment in the Southwest. Step into "a Moment Frozen in Time," as travelers from the 1930s await their boarding calls. Don't miss the steam locomotive rides on weekends.

Motorcycles

RODNEY C. GOTT MUSEUM
1425 Eden Road
York, Pennsylvania   17402
This museum offers a fabulous collection of early- and late-model motorcycles, including *Harley-Davidsons,* and Cal Rayborn's *XR-750,* the first bike to complete a 100-mile-per-hour lap at the Daytona International Speedway.

Roller Skates

NATIONAL MUSEUM OF ROLLER SKATING
Lincoln, Nebraska 68510
The world's largest collection of historical roller skates is housed in this museum. Also on exhibit are medals, photographs, films, costumes, and other treasures. Get up close and personal with the early skate designs and trace the history of roller skates.

Trucks

HALL OF FLAME
6101 East Van Buren
Phoenix, Arizona 85008
Here's where you'll find the world's largest and most complete collection of fire trucks and firefighting equipment. Also on exhibit are vintage helmets, uniforms, badges, and hundreds of items dating back to the 1800s. The restored "rigs" are not to be missed.

VAN HORN'S ANTIQUE TRUCK COLLECTION
3 miles north of Highway 65
Mason City, Iowa   50401
This museum is packed with antique trucks (built between 1909 and 1928) and truck memorabilia. One army truck was built in 1918 and has only 100 miles on it!

KEMP'S MACK TRUCK MUSEUM
Hillsboro, New Hampshire   03244
People from all over the U.S. and Canada go to see Dick Kemp's collection of more than 90 trucks. Among his treasures are 2 of the only 63 Mack trucks built in 1947 and the first truck he ever bought, a 1930 Bulldog Mack.

Seacraft

SUBMARINE FORCE LIBRARY AND MUSEUM
Naval Submarine Base New London
Groton, Connecticut   06349
Everything you ever wanted to know about submarines can be found in this official U.S. Naval museum. Exhibits include battle flags and pennants, submarine paintings, model submarines, photographs, artifacts from famous submarines, and *Nautilus,* the first nuclear-powered submarine to reach the North Pole.

Early submarine "Turtle" 1776

NEW BEDFORD WHALING MUSEUM
18 Johnny Cake Hill
New Bedford, Massachusetts   02740
This wonderful museum houses the largest U.S. collection of whaling items, paintings, shipboard gear, and whalebone carvings. Kids can hop aboard the largest ship model in the world, the 89-foot half-scale model *Lagoda*.

NATIONAL MARITIME MUSEUM
Hyde Street Pier
San Francisco, California   94109
Don't miss this huge collection of ships, including the beautiful square-rigger *Balcultha*. Also on exhibit are warplanes, model ships, and vintage steam machinery.

Spaceships and Rockets

MARSHALL SPACE FLIGHT CENTER
Alabama Space and Rocket Center
Huntsville, Alabama   35807
If you want to know what it's like to be launched into space, visit this museum. Kids can bounce around in the "Space Walker Jump," a device that simulates weightlessness; ride in a spinning theater that accelerates to 3-G, three times the force of gravity; and attend space movies and shows in the Space Dome Theater. You can also view the training center where kids attend Space Camp (see Chapter 1). Outside you're not likely to miss Shuttle and Rocket Park. There you'll see giant booster rockets and space shuttles.

JOHNSON SPACE CENTER
Houston, Texas   77058
What exactly goes on at Mission Control and how do astronauts train? You can find out by visiting this famous space center. Guided tours of Mission Control take place hourly, except, of course, when astronauts are in orbit. Self-guided tours include visits to the space museum, astronaut training facilities, lunar laboratories, and films and displays that tell the story of man and space.

NASA VISITORS CENTER
Ames Research Center
Moffett Field, California 94035
This center has the world's largest space shuttle wind-tunnel model, retired *U-2* aircraft, a *Mercury* space capsule, *Apollo* spacesuits, and exhibits that will teach you about astronautics and aeronautics. Don't miss the mock-up model of the *Galileo* Space Probe or the display of the futuristic NASP—the National Aerospace Plane.

Trolleys, Streetcars, and Carriages

SEASHORE TROLLEY MUSEUM
Log Cabin Road
Kennebunkport, Maine 04046
The world's largest collection of electric railway vehicles and streetcars is in this museum. Kids can watch workers as they restore vintage cars, and go for a ride on the museum's demonstration railway.

THE CARRIAGE MUSEUM
The Museums at Stony Brook
1208 Route 25A
Stony Brook, New York 11790
Every imaginable horse-drawn vehicle is displayed at this museum. All together there are more than 100, including sleighs, children's vehicles, sporting rigs, coaches, farm wagons, carriages, and firefighting equipment. You'll feel like you've stepped back in time.

CHAPTER 10

Fun Books
to Read

· ·

If you'd like to know more about your personal favorites, just hot-foot it to the nearest library and check out some or all of the following books.

Airplanes and Other Flying Machines

Airplanes of the Future
by Don Berliner
(Lerner Publications Co.,
  1987)

The Blimp Book
by George Larson
(Squarebooks, 1977)

Helicopters
by Graham Rickard
(Bookswright Press, 1987)

*The Smithsonian Book of Flight
  for Young People*
by Walter J. Boyne
(Atheneum, 1988)

Unusual Airplanes
by Don Berliner
(Lerner Publications Co., 1986)

Up, Up and Away! The Story of Ballooning
by Anabel Dean
(Westminster Press, 1980)

Bikes, Trikes, and Motorcycles

An Album of Motorcycle and Motorcycle Racing
by Elwood D. Baumann
(Franklin Watts Inc., 1982)

Better Bicycling for Boys and Girls
by George Sullivan
(Dodd, Mead & Co., 1984)

BMX Freestyle
by Larry Dane Brimner
(Franklin Watts Inc., 1987)

Chopper Cycle
by E. and R. S. Radlauer
(Franklin Watts Inc., 1972)

Trailbikes
by David Jefferies
(Franklin Watts Inc., 1984)

Cars

Dinosaur Cars
by John Struthers
(Lerner Publications, 1977)

*Encyclopedia Brown's Book
of Wacky Cars*
by Donald J. Sobol
(William Morrow, 1987)

*The Only Other Crazy
Car Book*
by Sloan Walker and
Andrew Vasey
(Walker & Co., 1984)

Veteran and Vintage Cars
by Peter Roberts
(Crescent Books, 1982)

Great Car Racing
by George Sullivan
(Dodd, Mead & Co., 1987)

Fun Vehicles
Just for Kids

Advanced Skate-Boarding
by LaVada Wier
(Wanderer Books, 1979)

Roller Skating
by D. J. Herda
(Franklin Watts Inc., 1979)

Skateboard
by Russ Howell
(Ure Smith, 1975)

Soap Box Derby Racing
by Sylvia A. Rosenthal
(Lothrop, Lee & Shepard,
1980)

The Way Things Work
by David Macaulay
(Houghton Mifflin Co., 1988)

Windsurfing
by Ross R. Olney
(Walker & Co., 1982)

Spaceships
and Rockets

America in Space
by Robin Kerrod
(Gallery Books, 1985)

Modern Spaceships
by Gregory Vogt
(Franklin Watts Inc., 1987)

Space Walks
by Wendy Walker
(Crescent Books, 1986)

Your Future in Space
Debra Schulke and Raymond
McPhee
(Crown, 1986)

Space Shuttle
by Michael Jay
(Franklin Watts Inc., 1984)

Trains

All Kinds of Trains
by Ron White
(Grosset & Dunlap, 1972)

*The Age of Mad Dragons: Steam
    Locomotives in North America*
by Douglas Waitley
(Beaufort Books, 1981)

The Big Book of Real Trains
by Walter Retan
(Grosset & Dunlap, 1987)

Railroads
by Bill Gunston
(Bookswright Press, 1988)

Trains
by Rixon Bucknal
(Grosset & Dunlap, 1973)

Trucks

Fire Trucks
by Hope Irvin Marston
(Dodd, Mead & Co., 1984)

*Monster Trucks and Other Giant
    Machines on Wheels*
by Jerry Bushey
(Carolrhoda Books Inc., 1985)

The Truck Book
by Robert L. Wolfe
(Carolrhoda Books Inc., 1981)

Trucks and Trucking
by Ruth and Mike Wolverton
(Franklin Watts Inc., 1982)

Trucks of Every Sort
by Ken Robbins
(Crown, 1981)

Ships, Submarines, and Other Floating Vessels

Freighters
by George Ancona
(Thomas Y. Crowell, 1985)

Mississippi Sternwheelers
by Pam and Gerry Zeck
(Carolrhoda Books Inc., 1982)

Ships
by N. S. Barrett
(Franklin Watts Inc., 1984)

Submarines
by Richard Humble
(Franklin Watts Inc., 1985)

Tugboat
by David Plowden
(Macmillian, 1976)

River Thrill Sports
by Andrew David and
    Tom Moran
(Dodd, Mead & Co., 1983)

Return of the Battleship
by George Sullivan
(Dodd, Mead & Co., 1983)

INDEX

....

Jumbo jets, 2, 47, 51, 56

Kneeboard, 233
Knievel, Evel, 209, 210
Kon Tiki, 178

LeMond, Greg, 205
License plates
    first to appear, 94
    first in U.S., 94
Lighthouses, 187
Lindbergh, Charles, 64
Locomotives
    first 100 mph run, 132
    first 200 mph run, 133
    first 300 mph run, 133
    first successful American, 132
    number in U.S., 135
    world's strongest, 137
    See also Railroads; Subways; Trains
Locomotives, steam powered,
    first successful, 6
    speeds of, 6
    world's fastest, 138
    world's largest, 138
Lunar rover, 33–34. *See also* Space
Lusitania, 176

Mayflower, 168, 194
Mission control. *See* Space
Monorail(s)
    at Disneyland, 135
    first, 2
    unique, 140–41
    See also Railroads; Trains
Morse Code, 178
Motocross, 205, 206. *See also* Bicycles;
    Motorcycles
Motorcycle(s), 208–13
    books about, 262
    earliest, 209
    first motorized, 209
    in firefighting, 127
    memorable, 212–13
    museums of, 256
    sidecars for, 209
    steam-powered, 208
Motorcycle racing
    enduro contests, 209
    famous race courses, 209, 212
    most dangerous races, 209

    most dangerous race course, 212
    superstars, 209, 210, 211
    TT racing, 209, 212
Motorcycle records
    fastest across the U.S., 212
    fastest speed, 210
    first 100 mph Daytona lap, 256
    longest jump, 210
    speed of, 209
    world's fastest, 210
Muldowney, Shirley, 108
Museums, 251–60. *See also specific
    vehicles*

Nautical
    measurements, 161
    nonsense, 158
    vocabulary, 168
Nautilus, 157, 195, 197
Navigation
    according to the Vikings, 154
    chronometer, 160, 161
    first compasses, 155
    periscope, 157
    sextant, 160, 161
    stern rudder, 156, 158
    See also Lighthouses

Ocean liners, 155, 165
    duties of, 175
    famous, 175, 176, 182
    largest ever built, 182
    speeds of, 6
    See also Ships

Paddlewheeler. *See* Steamboats
Parachute, 44, 46, 82
Parking lot, largest, 94
Parking meter, first, 93
Periscope, 157
Pilot(s)
    amazing kid, 52
    codes, 61–62
    flying aces, 45, 69, 70, 71
    Top-Gun training, 67–68
    See also Airplanes
Pirates, 169–72
Police
    cars for, 115–16
    motorcycles for, 213
"Pony Express," 7

The Kids' World

Once you have one Kids' World Almanac book...

THE KIDS' WORLD ALMANAC OF RECORDS AND FACTS
by Margo McLoone-Basta and Alice Siegel

THE SECOND KIDS' WORLD ALMANAC OF RECORDS AND FACTS
by Margo McLoone-Basta and Alice Siegel

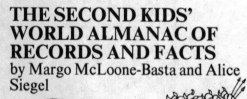

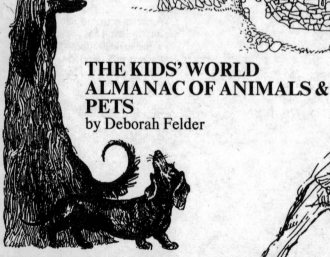

THE KIDS' WORLD ALMANAC OF ANIMALS & PETS
by Deborah Felder

THE KIDS' WORLD ALMANAC OF BASEBALL
by Thomas G. Aylesworth